LITERATURE AND THE TASTE OF
KNOWLEDGE

What does literature know? Does it offer us knowledge of its own or does it only interrupt and question other forms of knowledge? This book seeks to answer and to prolong these questions through the close examination of individual works and the exploration of a broad array of examples. Chapters on Henry James, Kafka, and the form of the villanelle are interspersed with wider-ranging enquiries into forms of irony, indirection and the uses of fiction, with examples ranging from Auden to Proust and Rilke, and from Calvino to Jean Rhys and Yeats. Literature is a form of pretence. But every pretence could tilt us into the real, and many of them do. There is no safe place for the reader: no literalist's haven where fact is always fact; and no paradise of metaphor, where our poems, plays and novels have no truck at all with the harsh and shifting world.

MICHAEL WOOD is the Charles Barnwell Straut Professor of English and Professor of Comparative Literature at Princeton University, and from 1995 to 2001 he was the Director of Gauss Seminars in Criticism at Princeton. He is a Fellow of the Royal Society of Literature and a Member of the American Philosophical Society. His works include books on Stendhal, García Márquez, Nabokov, Kafka and films. Additionally, he is a widely published essayist, with articles on film and literature in *London Review of Books*, *New York Review of Books*, *New York Times Book Review*, *New Republic* and other journals.

THE EMPSON LECTURES

The Empson Lectures, named after the great scholar and literary critic Sir William Empson (1906–84), have been established by the University of Cambridge as a series designed to address topics of broad literary and cultural interest. Sponsored jointly by the Faculty of English and Cambridge University Press, the series provides a unique forum for distinguished writers and scholars of international reputation to explore wide-ranging literary-cultural themes in an accessible manner.

LITERATURE AND THE TASTE OF KNOWLEDGE

MICHAEL WOOD

CAMBRIDGE
UNIVERSITY PRESS

CAMBRIDGE UNIVERSITY PRESS
Cambridge, New York, Melbourne, Madrid, Cape Town, Singapore, São Paulo

CAMBRIDGE UNIVERSITY PRESS
The Edinburgh Building, Cambridge CB2 2RU, UK
Published in the United States of America by Cambridge University Press, New York

www.cambridge.org
Information on this title: www.cambridge.org/9780521606530

© Michael Wood 2005

First published 2005

Printed in the United Kingdom at the University Press, Cambridge

A catalogue record for this book is available from the British Library

ISBN-13 978-0-521-84476-5 hardback
ISBN-10 0-521-84476-2 hardback
ISBN-13 978-0-521-60653-0 paperback
ISBN-10 0-521-60653-5 paperback

In memory of
F. W. Dupee
E. W. Said
J. P. Stern
and my father
teachers of thought and courage and care

'That is what comes of the taste for generalisation. You have only to hear nothing for a few days, in your hole, nothing but the sounds of things, and you begin to fancy yourself the last of human kind.'

Samuel Beckett, *Malone Dies*

'It does not even satisfy the understanding to stop living in order to understand.'

William Empson, *Seven Types of Ambiguity*

Contents

Acknowledgements

This book began life as the William Empson Lectures, given in Cambridge in October and November 2003, and I am deeply grateful to the University of Cambridge English Faculty and Cambridge University Press for the honour of their invitation. The occasion was a particular pleasure because I have always associated Empson, and my reading of *Seven Types of Ambiguity*, with my earliest sense of what criticism could really do – how much it could do, and how exciting it could be. Not that it's exciting all the time, or that the rest of us are Empson.

I wish to thank my Cambridge hosts Stefan Collini and John Kerrigan for their kindness, hospitality and intellectual support, and my Cambridge audiences for their intense attention and shrewd comments. I'm especially grateful to Gillian Beer, Pat Boyde, Martin Davies, Mary Jacobus, Hermione Lee, Robert Newsom, Jacqueline Rose and Sheila Stern, whose advice and insight improved this book in so many ways. I learnt a great deal from Angela Leighton's wonderful British Academy Lecture 'Elegies of Form in Bishop, Plath, Stevenson', which she kindly sent to me.

I gave an early version of one of the lectures at a seminar at Yale in September 2003, and gained much from the lively responses to it, in particular from those of Dudley Andrew, Wai-Chee Dimock, Paul Fry, Amy Hungerford, Annabel

Patterson and Linda Peters. And then there are traces in this book of more conversations than I can count. I should like to mention, as emblems of so many others, my talks long and short with Rita Copeland, Stanley Corngold, Jeff Dolven, Hal Foster, Claudia Johnson, Mark Johnson, Jeff Nunokawa, Philip Pettit, Jonathan Steinberg, Susan Stewart, David Wallace, Gillian White and C. K. Williams.

I have added to the text here and there, filling out discussions and examples, and I have tried to get rid of some of the wilder inconsistencies. I have modified the conversational tone where it wouldn't translate on to the page, and dropped the local jokes where they wouldn't travel beyond the Fens. But I have tried to maintain the pace and style of the lectures, their sense of ongoing speculation and often surprised discovery, their conjuring of questions in rather restless dialogue with further questions.

Last but far from least, I should like to thank Sarah Stanton for all her thoughtful help in putting this book together, and Libby Willis for her delicate copy-editing and the inspired example of an alternative meaning on p. 110.

Princeton
May 2005

Introduction: *Among the analogies*

In her poem 'At the Fishhouses' Elizabeth Bishop contemplates
the cold, clear water of a northern sea. She says she has

> seen it over and over, the same sea, the same,
> slightly, indifferently swinging above the stones,
> icily free above the stones,
> above the stones and then the world.

She has seen it and she tells us what it would be like to touch
it ('your wrist would ache immediately . . . and your hand
would burn'). And then what it would be like to taste it:

> If you tasted it, it would first taste bitter,
> then briny, then surely burn your tongue.
> It is like what we imagine knowledge to be.

This is not quite an imagination of knowledge, only of what
knowledge resembles, but we sense the appeal and the severity
of the claim immediately. Bishop's analogue for knowledge is
'dark, salt, clear, moving, utterly free,/drawn from the cold
hard mouth/of the world', and 'our knowledge' itself is, she
says, 'historical, flowing, and flown'.[1]

---

[1] Elizabeth Bishop, *The Complete Poems*. New York: Farrar, Straus and
Giroux, 1979, pp. 65–66

We may want to associate knowledge, as many poets have, with southern lands rather than northern seas, and we may want to leave geography and metaphor behind, locating knowledge only in the minds of animals, especially humans. But whatever we do, as long as we don't let go of the project entirely, we shall have made a move towards the double subject of this book: the act of representing knowledge, especially elusive knowledge, in words; and the nature of the knowledge that literary arrangements of words can offer us.

But does literature offer us knowledge? It certainly represents it, as we have just seen. But a representation is, by definition, not the thing itself, and both literature and knowledge are words worth using carefully. There are all kinds of treasures which are not knowledge, and we should not betray them by giving them the wrong name.

The worry about the relation between literature and knowledge is a very old one, and it's not getting any younger. When Dorothy Walsh, in an elegant book called *Literature and Knowledge*, published in 1969, said the worry was old, she meant it went back at least to Plato. When Stathis Gourgouris says it is old, in a recent book called *Does Literature Think?*, he means the same thing. 'The idea that literature might harbor its own mode of knowledge is ancient, at least as old as the so-called quarrel between poetry and philosophy and Plato's notorious expulsion of the poets from the city in the *Republic*. It is fair to say that since Plato's famous decision there has been an implicit but consistent association of the poetic act with a peculiar, mysterious, and even dangerous sort of knowledge.'[2] Actually, even Socrates, who was the one making the decision, thought

---

[2] Stathis Gourgouris, *Does Literature Think?* Stanford: Stanford University Press, 2003, p. 2

the worry was old, and apologized for his dismissal of poetry by saying, 'But in case we are charged with a certain harshness and lack of sophistication, let's also tell poetry that there is an ancient quarrel between it and philosophy.'[3]

But Plato's worry is not ours, and indeed our worry, in 2005, is perhaps not quite the worry we might have had, did have, in 1969. This is one of the things it means to possess knowledge that is 'historical, flowing, and flown'. Or if the question we are asking is the same – to quote Dorothy Walsh, 'What kind of knowledge, if any, does literary art afford?', or more delicately, 'Do works of literary art, when functioning successfully as such, have any intimate engagement with what may be called knowledge?' – our reasons for asking it are different, and so is our idea of what might constitute an interesting answer. Walsh thought that the disengagement of literature from direct knowledge claims might 'be seen as the liberation of literature from the alien and extraneous burden of cognitive concern. So liberated, literature is free to develop its potentialities strictly as art.' The opposite view, she suggested, was not engagement with direct knowledge but a different sense of disengagement, the view that 'the disengagement provides the opportunity for the recognition of the distinctive kind of cognitive significance literary art can have'. 'Shall we see the disengagement as the liberation of Ariel?' Walsh asked. 'Or . . . shall we say that the magic island . . . cannot be abandoned and that the control of Prospero over both Ariel and Caliban must be sustained?'[4] I don't think many people are recommending

---

[3] Plato, *Republic*. Translated by C. M. A. Grube. Indianapolis: Hackett, 1992, p. 278

[4] Dorothy Walsh, *Literature and Knowledge*. Middletown: Wesleyan University Press, 1969, pp. 3, 11, 15, 30.

the liberation of Ariel these days, or a picture of literature 'strictly as art', and I don't wish to recommend them myself. But I do want to wonder, as Walsh did, whether the only alternative is total submission to Prospero.

The question that drives this book is an oldish one for me personally. At one time, around 1960, when I was trying to disentangle art from other human affairs, I would have said literature doesn't know anything and can't know anything. Literature is a form of play, and it plays at knowing as it plays at all kinds of other activities. It is infinitely valuable, but valuable as play, not as disguised or sweetened work. I now think that this formulation, and others like it, are ways of asking the question rather than answering it, and over the years I have found the question more and more puzzling. This is in part because I no longer want to disentangle art from other human affairs, only to understand its entanglement in them. Still, literature does make very special calls on us, and the question assumed a new shape for me a couple of years ago. The scene was a colloquium on the role of doubt in the human sciences, and all the participants – anthropologists, political scientists, historians, literary scholars and others – spoke happily in praise of doubt: as a precaution, a necessary modesty of method. Without doubt, they said, there can be no knowledge. But they also thought the doubting had to stop. Once we have exercised all the proper degrees of doubt, they suggested, we can give it up, and deliver the knowledge we have secured.

This seems to me an admirable, even indispensable programme for the advancement of learning, but it doesn't come close to describing what happens in the writing and reading and close study of literature. Literature, I wanted to say, isn't like this, it's the place where doubt never ends. But this isn't right. In fact, it's dangerously wrong. The entertainment of possibilities in literature – and literature, in one crucial aspect, just is the entertainment of possibilities – resembles doubting, and is probably a good school for informed doubt. But it is not doubt, precisely because, in literature, alternatives are in play but not in contention.[5] We are interested not in the choices we are going to make but in the choices we could make, and we can always go back on our interpretative decisions. Indeed, we shall be better readers if we do go back on them, and there is no equivalent in practical life for the sheer, disinterested attraction of this multiplication of chances.

It's true that in many applications of literature – on the stage or the screen – certain decisions are made which cannot be reversed and so form part of the life of the director or the actor. Once you have settled on the intonation with which Lear and Cordelia are to say the word 'nothing', on the exact degree or mixture of anger, innocence, outrage, bewilderment, stubbornness and whatever else you want, there is no going back when the word is said, the die is cast. But the text remains, like a musical score, always ready

---

[5] Cf William Empson, *Seven Types of Ambiguity*. New York: New Directions, 1966, pp. 81–82. 'The conservative attitude to ambiguity is curious and no doubt wise; it allows a structure of associated meanings to be shown in a note, but not to be admitted; the reader is encouraged to swallow the thing by a decent reserve; it is thought best not to let him know he is thinking in such a complicated medium . . . Here as in recent atomic physics there is a shift in progress, which tends to attach the notion of a probability to the natural object rather than to the fallibility of the human mind . . . We must conclude either that a great deal has been added to Shakespeare by the mere concentration upon him of wrong-headed literary attention, or that his original meaning was of a complexity to which we must work our way back, and which we may as well acknowledge without attempting to drape ourselves in a transparent chain of negatives.'

for another, quite different performance. Kafka wrote that the unalterability of the text is the commentators' despair,[6] but we could register the same perception in another light, and think of the text as having a strange ability to survive all alterations. And it's not hard to imagine that a source of theological despair could be the basis of a certain moral freedom, whereby we actively conjugate what is with what might be. Literature, like doubt, will not let knowledge rest; but not because it loves only doubt or doesn't care for knowledge.

This proposition owes more than a little to Wittgenstein's extraordinary sequence of meditations on what happens when we seem to find ourselves seeing and thinking at the same time, as when we recognize the first and then the second aspect of an optical puzzle, or suddenly realize we know someone we hadn't at once remembered. 'I *see* that it has not changed.' And again, 'The expression of change of aspect is the expression of a *new* perception and at the same time of the perception's being unchanged.' The riddle for the philosopher is that he regards thinking as an action and seeing as a condition. How can an experience be made up of both elements at once? 'How is it possible to *see* an object according to an *interpretation*?' Literature doesn't answer this question, but it does enact the riddle constantly, offering what seem to be direct perceptions intricately entwined with often elaborate interpretations. It does this so constantly that we can hardly speak of a riddle any more. 'When it looks as if there were no room for such a form

---

[6] Franz Kakfa, *Der Proceß*, Frankfurt: Fischer, 1993, p. 234. Translated by Breon Mitchell. New York: Schocken Books, 1998, p. 220. '*Die Schrift ist unveränderlich und die Meinungen sind oft nur ein Ausdrück der Verzweiflung darüber*'. ('The text is immutable, and the opinions are often only an expression of despair over it.') Over the fact of immutability, that is.

between other ones,' Wittgenstein says, 'you have to look for it in another dimension.'[7]

I'm deeply in agreement with Paul Fry's argument about the suspension of knowledge in literature, the moments of what he calls 'ostension' in which people and things are held in their nonsignifying opacity.[8] Without such moments there would be no literature. But a multiplication can produce an effect very similar to that of a suspension, and I see now that I am mainly trying to explore the unsettling of direct knowledge by other knowledges; and the return of knowledge after its suspension. I also share Derek Attridge's sense of the singularity of literature, its restlessness and its resistance to rules. And yet Attridge himself says that he 'almost' wishes to accept the argument that literary works are not to be distinguished from others, even if he adds that this 'almost' is the subject of his book.[9] Literature is a name for a set of extraordinary achievements in words, but there is also something admirably ordinary about the literary impulse, something we find in the slightest hints and verbal gestures of ordinary life, whenever we speak playfully or ironically, or call something by a name that is not its own; whenever we see or say that people and places have markedly changed while stubbornly, loyally remaining the same.

[7] Ludwig Wittgenstein, *Philosophical Investigations*. Translated by G. E. M. Anscombe. Oxford: Blackwell, 1967, pp. 193, 196, 200. Wittgenstein's italics.
[8] Paul Fry, *A Defense of Poetry*. Stanford: Stanford University Press, 1995, p. 13 and passim. 'Ostension ... is that indicative gesture toward reality which precedes and underlies the construction of meaning ... it is the deferral of knowledge by the disclosure, as a possibility, that existence can be meaning-*free*.'
[9] Derek Attridge, *The Singularity of Literature*. London: Routledge, 2004, p. 10.

There is an excellent focus for the old and new question, a brilliant brief statement of its current force, and a way of holding the whole issue before our minds, in Peter de Bolla's book *Art Matters*. De Bolla is looking at a Barnett Newman painting (*Vir Heroicus Sublimis*) in the Museum of Modern Art in New York. He has decided that the usual critical questions – what does this painting mean?, what is it trying to say? – are the wrong ones. He offers one or two not all that appealing alternatives ('how does this painting determine my address to it?, how does it make me feel?, what does it make me feel?') and says that 'beyond these questions lies the insistent murmur of great art, the nagging thought that the work holds something to itself, contains something that in the final analysis remains untouchable, unknowable'. Then de Bolla arrives at what I find the truly haunting question: 'What does this painting know?'[10]

The question has two immediate and very interesting implications. First, that a painting might know something that the painter didn't. And second, that the painting probably knows a lot that it is not going to tell us. I'm interested in the murmur of small art as well as great art – I think small art may know things, too – and I want to put the question to literature rather than to painting, but the question is the same. To frame it rather schematically, thinking of Proust and asthma, say, we could ask, not what Proust knew about the condition or what doctors know now or knew in Proust's time, but what *A la recherche du temps perdu* knows about asthma – what it knows and perhaps will not tell us directly, or what it knows that only novels know, or only this novel knows. Many see dangers in such personification – the novel

[10] Peter de Bolla, *Art Matters*. Cambridge: Harvard University Press, 2001, p. 31.

is not a person and can't know anything, only novelists and readers can – but for the moment I should like this form of the question, and the figure of speech, just to hang in the air, like an old tune, or the memory of a mood.

There is something unavoidably oblique about literature. It could always say, like Salman Rushdie's narrator in *Shame*, 'My story, my fictional country exist, like myself, at a slight angle to reality.'[11] Sometimes the angle is not at all slight. Yet, strangely enough, as I have already suggested, we meet this obliquity head on. Dorothy Walsh concludes that 'literary art, when functioning successfully as literary art, provides knowledge in the form of realization: the realization of what anything might come to as a form of lived experience'.[12] This is very well put, and much of what I have to say is merely a gloss on this claim. But literature not only reports on what happens and on what may happen, it is itself 'a form of lived experience'. We have the direct experience of words behaving and misbehaving. Our reading is an immediate event, like tasting salt or coriander.

Roland Barthes says that literature is found wherever words have savour, and he tells us that the French words for knowledge and savour (*savoir* and *saveur*) have the same etymology in Latin. My scholarly friends laugh at this claim, and I don't doubt their grounds. By my ear reminds me that in Spanish the words not only share a false etymology but are still the same – '*quién sabe?*' is 'who knows?', and '*a qué sabe?*' is 'what does it taste of? – and so I find the connection hard to shake off. Barthes continues, 'Where knowledge is concerned, things must, if they are to become what they are, what they have been, have that ingredient,

---

[11] Salman Rushdie, *Shame*. London: Picador, 1984, p. 29.
[12] Walsh, *Literature and Knowledge*, p. 136.

the salt of words. It is this taste of words which makes knowledge profound, fecund.'[13] The knowledge Barthes has in mind is distinctly the knowledge found in literature, and I shall return to his intricate thoughts on this topic. What is particularly interesting here, and neatly clarified by the metaphor of taste, is the proposition that things have their present and past life in words, that in words they become what they are, which is already a paradox, like slouching towards Bethlehem to be born, and also become what they have been. We could translate 'this taste of words' as 'this taste for words' and thereby shift the activating of knowledge slightly from language towards the person.

There are two other sets of meanings I hope the notion of taste may discreetly evoke. If the taste of words offers knowledge, if literature gives us a taste of knowledge, this can only be a taste, a sample, rather than an elaborate or plentiful meal. We are going to have to go elsewhere for the continuous main course. And if we directly face literature's obliquity in one sense, it's important that we respect its indirection in another, because the relation between literature and knowledge is always complex.

And then who could forget the most famous association of tasting and knowledge in the Western and Near Eastern world? God tells our first ancestor that if he eats of the tree of good and evil he will 'surely die', but there is another narrative. 'And the Serpent said unto the woman, Ye shall not surely die. For God doth know, that in the day ye eat thereof, then your eyes shall be opened: and ye shall be as

[13] Roland Barthes, *Leçon*. Paris: Seuil, 1978, p. 21. Translated by Richard Howard in *A Barthes Reader*, ed. Susan Sontag. London: Jonathan Cape, 1982, p. 465

gods, knowing good and evil.'[14] The serpent is wrong about death and the chance of being like gods but right, as it happens, about God's knowledge and the knowledge to be had by humans. It does not diminish the religious status of this text to see it as also fully literary, making imaginative options concrete, and reminding us of some of the stakes of knowing.

Of course, there are many who deny the relevance or importance of literature, who believe that its knowledge, if it has any, is trivial or merely decorative. A brutal and one-sided answer to this objection is to mention some of the damage literature has done. But I wish more generally to put back into play, as Gourgouris does, the relation between elusive knowledge, or even a story of knowledge, and danger, even mortality. Sometimes a taste is enough to get you evicted, as in Genesis, or worse than evicted, as in Julio Cortázar's eerie story, 'Continuity of Parks', where a person is murdered (or about to be murdered) by a character in the novel he is reading.

I have tried in this book both to give some individual answers to my general question and to keep the question itself alive by renewed asking and more examples. I'm sure the examples are more important (and more fun) than the question; but I hope the question is something more than an excuse for the examples. I have suggested, in Chapters One, Three and Five, what particular forms of knowledge in literature may look like, or taste like: the knowledge of the very gap between knowledge and life, between what can be said and what can't; of what takes the place of thinking when we encounter or engineer the unthinkable; of an array of scarcely nameable forms of loss and regret. And I have

---

[14] Genesis 3: 4–5.

continued to wonder, in Chapters Two, Four and Six, whether knowledge is the right word for what we keep meeting in literature: in an irony that comes, as Henry James said, from having so much imagination rather than too little;[15] in hypothetical affirmations, instructions and questions that don't necessarily remain hypothetical, in jokes and analogies that are not only jokes and analogies; in fictions that have taken up residence in reality, and in the circumstantial history of what hasn't happened. I'm sure knowledge is the right word for all practical and political purposes, where nothing less will do, and I don't want to disavow it. But I do believe there is value in hesitating before we settle on it, and throughout the whole book, even in the chapters that unequivocally claim knowledge for literature, I have sought to remain loyal to this hesitation, whose other name, I believe, is not indecision or undecidability but patience.

[15] Henry James, 'The Jolly Corner', in *Selected Tales*, ed. Peter Messent/ Tom Paulin. London: Everyman, 1983, p. 360. 'Her smile had for him ... an irony without bitterness and that came, exactly, from her having so much imagination – not, like the cheap sarcasms with which one heard most people ... bid for the reputation of cleverness, from nobody's really having any.'

CHAPTER I

What Henry knew

I

My slightly frivolous chapter title takes us straight to Henry James, of course, and the joke is meant to indicate, among other things, that I recognize how obvious a move this is, once we have started on the question of literature and knowledge.[1] It was James who wrote so eloquently, in relation to the publication of Flaubert's letters, of 'the insurmountable desire to *know*', and who thought, in that context, that 'some day or other we shall surely agree that . . . we pay

---

[1] I had written this chapter when I came across Cynthia Ozick's earlier use of the joke (with a looser rhythmic echo) in the introduction and the title essay of her book *What Henry James Knew*. What Henry James knew, for Ozick, 'was the nobility of art', although characteristically James himself had put it in the negative: 'I know of no substitute whatever for the force and beauty of its process.' Ozick nicely says that 'hidden knowings are everywhere' in late James. My particular point in this chapter is that active hiding from knowledge is everywhere in *The Wings of the Dove*. I am happy, too, to have Ozick's company in the use of the trope suggesting a book may know more than its author does, or may know different things. '*The Castle*, for example,' she writes, 'appears to know more than Kafka himself knows – more about its own matter and mood, more about its remonstrances and motives, more about the thread of Kafka's mind.' And, 'It is probable that *The Awkward Age* is a novel that knows far more than its author knew, and holds more secrets of panic, shame, helplessness, and chaos than James could candidly face.' *What Henry James Knew*. London: Jonathan Cape, 1993, pp. 2, 132, 102, 133.

more for some kinds of knowledge than those particular kinds are worth'. But to read these words, and to think of the knowledge at issue – the fact, as James says, 'that the author of calm, firm masterpieces ... was narrow and noisy'[2] – is to remember how many kinds of knowledge there are, how much work the words *know* and *knowledge* are so often asked to do, and how varied that work is.

If we read the actual sentence I have massacred for my title, for instance, at the point in the novel from which James takes his phrase, we come upon another kind of knowledge entirely: not the goal of curiosity but the fruit of experience. In his preface to *What Maisie Knew*, James writes of the appeal for the novelist of a child's 'confused and obscure notation' of a tangle of adult relations, namely the goings on of her divorced parents and their changing companions, and adds that it was important for him that Maisie should see more than she understood. 'Small children have many more perceptions than they have terms to translate them.' And not only small children, as I shall suggest later. 'She has', James says of Maisie, 'the wonderful importance of shedding a light far beyond any reach of her comprehension.'[3] This is clear enough, and James's remarks are of great technical interest. But the text of the novel itself is more ambiguous, precisely because of the strong and multiple valences of the word *know*. Do Maisie's perceptions shed 'a light far beyond any reach of her comprehension'? Well, perhaps not beyond *any* reach. Just beyond the reach we are likely to assign to it. But is that the right reach? The novel is not called *What Maisie*

---

[2] Henry James, 'Gustave Flaubert', in *Selected Literary Criticism*, ed. Morris Shapira. Cambridge: Cambridge University Press, 1981, pp. 139–140.
[3] Henry James, 'Preface', *What Maisie Knew*. London: Penguin, 1966, pp. 9, 11.

Saw, or *What Maisie Failed to Understand*. The whole beauty of the thing is that we can't know for sure what Maisie knows. Tony Tanner has said that 'in a sense the book hinges on what Maisie does *not* know'[4] – especially what she doesn't know about sex. But by the same token she can, as Tanner also suggests, deeply know all kinds of things without knowing the basic facts. Right at the end of the book, the governess Mrs Wix gives Maisie a piece of information about the whereabouts of two of the errant adults. Maisie says, 'Oh I know.' James then writes, 'Mrs Wix gave a sidelong look. She still had room for wonder at what Maisie knew.'[5]

We still have room for wonder at what James knew – and in the light of our question about literature and knowledge, at what James's novels know. And I hope my chapter title, if viewed suspiciously enough, may help us discreetly to ask whether James and his novels know quite the same things. I want to use a great novel by James to explore some of the working meanings of the notion of knowledge; and I want, at the same time, to use the notion of knowledge to open up a great novel in what I hope is a fresh way. The novel is *The Wings of the Dove*, first published in 1902. This novel seems to know a lot about knowledge, and especially about knowledge and words, and about knowledge and novels.

II

It will help to clear the ground a little if we look briefly at some of the ostensive definitions of knowledge the novel handily

[4] Tony Tanner, *Henry James: The Writer and his Work*. Amherst: University of Massachusetts Press, 1985, p. 89.
[5] James, *What Maisie Knew*, p. 248.

offers us. They correspond to, but also complicate, the *OED*'s
central definitions, especially the ones that pertain to knowledge
by experience or personal acquaintance, knowledge as awareness of the facts, and knowledge as an understanding of pat-
terns of relations or connection. For the sake of convenience,
and following the tutelary spirit of William Empson, I've
grouped the meanings of knowledge in *The Wings of the
Dove* in seven sets.

One. In this novel you can know that something is the
case. This is the most frequent meaning of the words know
and knowledge. You could know, for instance, although you
don't, what terrible disgraceful thing your father has done.
In the opening pages of the novel, Kate Croy is waiting for
her elegant but seedy dad, and James's prose is at its insi-
dious best. Lionel Croy is, we learn, 'a terrible husband not
to live with'. 'Those who knew him a little said "How he
does dress!" – those who knew him better said "How *does*
he?" 'Nothing ... was more wonderful than what he sometimes would take for offence, unless it might be what he
sometimes wouldn't.' Late in the book Kate says of him that
he is 'never ill'. 'He's a marvel. He's only – endless.'⁶ What's
important here is that the possibility of simple if disagreeable
knowledge is mentioned only because it is so resolutely
refused – a pattern which comes up again and again in the
novel. 'Whatever it was that was horrid ... that he had
done,' the wife and daughters think, 'thank God they
didn't really know' [60]. A little later Merton Densher, the
man Kate is in love with, asks her just what it is her father has
been up to.

⁶ Henry James, *The Wings of the Dove*. London: Penguin, 1986, pp. 60, 58,
64, 494. All further quotations from this novel are taken from this edition
and are indicated in brackets on the page.

'What has he done, if no one can name it?'
'He has done everything.'
'Oh – everything ! Everything's nothing.'
'Well then,' said Kate, 'he has done some particular thing. It's known – only, thank God, not to us' [99].

Kate recalls her mother telling her – Kate was about fifteen – that if she hears anything against her father she is to 'remember it's perfectly false'. 'That was the way I knew it was true,' [99] Kate adds without missing a beat.

In this same sense of knowledge, and in this same novel – I'm listing only instances where James himself uses the words know or knowledge – you could (and do) know what your material circumstances add up to, what your aunt's position in the world means. You could (and do) know that your young friend lacks culture, needs to broaden her horizon by travel. You could (and later do) know that she is ill. You could (and do) know that you yourself are ill. You could (and nearly everybody in the book does) know a particular fact or set of facts, a secret, something that others don't know.

Two. You can, if they tell you, know what other people think, and if you are willing to contemplate it, you can know what you yourself feel or believe. It is in this sense that Kate Croy's sister tells Kate that she wants her to know how unfavourably she views Merton Densher, and it is in this same sense that Densher knows he will never be rich. Or more precisely, he knows how firmly he believes he will never be rich. 'His conviction on this head was in truth quite positive and a thing by itself; he failed, after analysis, to understand it, though he had naturally more lights on it than anyone else. He knew it subsisted in spite of an equal consciousness of his being neither mentally nor physically quite helpless . . . he knew it to be absolute, though secret, and also, strange to say, about common undertakings, not discouraging, not prohibitive' [95].

Three. You can know people, in the sense of having been introduced to them. It is in this context that two Americans in the novel disembark at Dover, 'completely unknown . . . amid the completely unknowing' [142]. There are of course other suggestions lurking there, too: of stealth, on the visitors' part; of unpreparedness, on the part of the home team. You can know, in the sense of being acquainted with, certain social refinements, and a character asserts, with some show of truth in the particular context, that 'men *don't* know' about such things. Or rather, 'They know in such matters almost nothing but what women show them' [120]. We are still within the same range of meanings when we are told that a suave and ultimately rather sinister English aristocrat has given up discriminations 'from too much knowledge'. Well, strictly we are told that 'he spoke as if he had' given up discriminations from too much knowledge [150–151]. And if you can know too much about the world, you can also know too little, as the young American visitor in conversation with this man obviously does. Yet she is the person who beautifully complicates just this sense of knowledge by making it modulate towards some of its more interesting meanings. She says to this man (they are at a dinner in high-to-middling English society), 'You all here know each other – I see that – as far as you know anything. You know what you're used to, and it's your being used to it . . . that makes you. But there are things you don't know' [158]. The young woman has another interesting perception. If these people all know each other but still can't place Kate Croy – 'if the handsome girl's place among them was something even their initiation couldn't deal with' – then Kate must 'indeed be a quantity' [161].

Four. You can know people, and things, in the sense of recognising them, and this is what happens when Milly Theale, the young American I have just been quoting, happens to be in the National Gallery in London and catches sight of someone she has met in New York – the already mentioned Merton Densher. She looks at his bared head – he has taken his hat off to mop his brow – and is 'shaken by a knowledge of it' [242]. As a matter of narrative information this phrase means only that she is surprised to see him, but of course we soon learn that she is shaken because she knows him well enough to like him a lot, but not well enough to know what to do with her liking.

Five. You can know people or fail to know them, in the sense of deep intimacy – this is not the most frequent sense of knowledge in the novel, but it may be the most important. Several people insist, for example, that Milly is not 'easy to know', and Kate says, paradoxically, that it's hard to know her because it's so easy to see her. 'One *sees* her with intensity – sees her more than one sees almost anyone; but then one discovers that that isn't knowing her' [276]. And in a terrible piece of deception and self-deception, a lie which turns into a truth, Densher tells Millie that he doesn't feel as if he knows Kate – 'really to call know' [305]. He is in love with her and planning to marry her, but he doesn't know her. We get a glimpse of the lie and the truth in such a comment when, right at the end of the novel, we are told that he sees in his and Kate's embrace 'the need to bury in the dark blindness of each other's arms the knowledge of each other that they couldn't undo' [500]. What could have brought these likeable people to such a pass?

Six. There recurs in the book, and in much of James, an interesting, semi-intransitive sense of 'know', where the word seems almost synonymous with life, or at least with

vivid consciousness. 'She hadn't cared,' we read of the young
American woman, 'she had too much wanted to know' [235].
Wanted to know what? Particular things about the world, of
course. But also everything. Earlier in the book two lovers
are said to have between them 'somehow everything to feel
and to know' [89]. Densher would not suggest in this context
that everything is nothing, although with such scope and
such ambitions, if one failed to know and feel everything,
one might feel one was left with nothing.

Seven. There is a sense of knowing as simply meaning
guessing right. 'She knew', a character in the novel says of
another. 'She knew.' The knowledge in question has to do
with a visit to a doctor. When challenged, the person says
she knows only that the other character saw something.
'When I say she knows I should say she's a person who
guesses' [313, 314]. Is this knowledge? Strictly it can't be. A
guess is a guess, right or wrong. But of course guesses do
connect with the realm of knowledge when they are right,
and I'm not sure that the temptation to say we knew, when
we were only guessing with deep conviction, has to be
resisted in every case. I agree that the sense of what we
usually mean by knowledge would have to be expanded a
little – but why not?

III

The shabbiness of Kate Croy's father is a pure delight, but
I dwelt on it for other reasons, too. Because his case represents the first of several mysteries in the novel, zones where
knowledge is available but refused or hidden, and because
his daughter does not, in the end, escape his seedy shadow.
For all the clarity of her heart and mind, her high courage,
her being such a 'quantity', as Millie thinks, Kate ends up on

just the shifting moral ground where we imagine her father to be so nastily at home. She herself is not shifting; she is magnificently firm. But the ground gets very marshy around her, and she bears her responsibility for that. Kate has a design that, as Dorothea Krook says, is 'a miracle of intelligence, courage, good sense, good will – everything in fact that the world ever asks of any worldly design, provided that it succeeds'.[7] And if it doesn't succeed? And who determines success and failure in such intricate cases?

What is the case? Most of the pieces of it lie before us in the passages I have already quoted. Let's put the pieces together. Kate Croy, anxious to separate herself from her father's shame, to give what she calls the 'broken sentence' of her family's life 'a sort of meaning' [57], and at the same time to avoid the penury and meanness of her sister's married and then widowed state, has allowed herself to be taken up by her rich Aunt Maud. Maud admires Kate greatly, and wants to marry her off to some grandee, or, failing a really grand grandee, the sinister aristocrat I mentioned earlier as in conversation with Milly. His name is Lord Mark. Kate has other plans. She is love with Densher and won't marry anyone else. But she won't marry him as long as he is poor, and she has Aunt Maud's wishes to contend with. Her idea is that it must be possible to have money and marry whom she wants – she just doesn't know how. Perhaps Aunt Maud will come round to the idea of Densher. No point in giving up yet.

Enter Milly Theale, the young American, and her travelling companion Susan Stringham, an old friend of Aunt

---

[7] Dorothea Krook, *The Ordeal of Consciousness in Henry James*. Cambridge: Cambridge University Press, 1967, p. 215.

Maud, it turns out. Milly is immensely rich, and James really goes to town on the topic.

> It prevailed even as the truth of truths that the girl couldn't get away from her wealth . . . She couldn't dress it away, nor walk it away, nor read it away, nor think it away; she could neither smile it away in any dreamy absence nor blow it away in any softened sigh. She couldn't have lost it if she had tried – that was what it was to be really rich. It had to be *the* thing you were. [133]

Milly is also very ill, in fact dying, and I have always wanted to believe that her wealth is her illness, that in a furiously compressed parable James is telling us not that money is the root of all evil but something scarier: that the combination of real wealth and real innocence is mortal, that the mere promise of unconditioned, uncalculating possibility is enough to bring down, as if by magic, the trap of what James calls, in this novel, 'the offensive real' [352], also described as 'the chill of the losing game' [351]. But in fact he is saying, or his novel is saying, something rather more complicated.

We never get to know what Millie's illness is. Susan Stringham doesn't want to know, and recognizes only that it isn't what Milly thought it was. 'She's wrong – she hasn't what she thought.' The great doctor Sir Luke Strett examined her 'for what she supposed' but found 'something else' [320, 321]. It's a relief to know he examined her, because he mostly seems to diagnose by talking like an oracle, and by giving Jamesian advice about 'living'. Milly thinks he finds things out 'simply by his genius', and you have to read very carefully to discover a discreet mention of 'much interrogation, auscultation, exploration, much noting of his own sequences and neglecting of hers' [211]. I think that's an examination. Kate believes the illness can't be tuberculosis.

'Isn't consumption, taken in time, now curable?' [283]. But perhaps Milly's illness is not 'taken in time'. In any event, it is clear that Sir Luke thinks her plight has an element of 'option' or 'volition' about it [213, 214], and that happiness and love would be good for Milly. Would they prolong her life? The suggestion is repeatedly made, but perhaps all anyone means is that if her life is full it will matter less how short it is.

At this point a ghastly conspiracy arises. Two ghastly conspiracies. Kate and Densher decide that if they deny or hide their love for each other, he can pay court to Milly, and see what comes of it. Well, he won't even have to pay court, only allow the girl to love him. They spell out the implications of their plan down to the last detail. If necessary, Densher is to marry Milly. 'So that' – he puts it as a question – 'when her death has taken place I shall in the natural course have money?' Kate assents. 'You'll in the natural course have money. We shall in the natural course be free.' A moment later he says, 'What I don't make out is how, caring for me, you can like it.' Kate says, 'I don't like it, but I'm a person, thank goodness, who can do what I don't like' [394–395].

In the other conspiracy, Aunt Maud and Susan Stringham decide that Densher will be good for Milly, like some extraordinary fortifying medicine, and are undeterred by their certain knowledge of his and Kate's commitment to each other. Aunt Maud is very firm. 'Kate thinks she cares. But she's mistaken' [323–324]. Maud means that Milly doesn't have to be told about Kate's supposed mistake, and that Densher therefore does not count as spoken for. It doesn't matter what Kate feels if no one mentions it; and although Maud and Susan Stringham don't know it, Kate herself is busy giving exactly the same impression to Milly – namely that she doesn't care at all for Densher.

Milly and Susan have gone to Venice, and everyone visits them there. Densher stays on and pays his passive, dilatory court to Milly, his whole idea of honour attached to the idea that he has not actually lied about anything. When Kate says at one stage that they have told too many lies to back out now, he insists that he hasn't told any. Then Lord Mark, having briefly pursued Milly to Venice in order to propose to her (in vain) and returned to London to propose to Kate (also in vain), puts two and two together and tells Milly the whole shabby story, the fact of Densher's and Kate's longstanding and unbroken engagement. Milly loses the will to live , and 'has turned her face to the wall' [421]. There is an excruciating scene between Susan and Densher in which she asks him to deny, if he can, the revelation Lord Mark made to Milly. Densher has one last interview with Milly but he doesn't deny the revelation. In that interview, we later learn, he felt 'forgiven, dedicated, blessed' [469] by Milly, and she writes him a letter which reaches him just before Christmas, and at the very time of her death.

Milly's fate, William Righter astutely suggests, is a modern tragedy because of its 'deep and terrifying emptiness'; because 'it is not the result of things that happen to her but of things that don't'. 'The absence of emotional fulfilment', Righter continues, 'is a precise area of Jamesian knowledge.'[8] The precision is not in doubt but this is surely a strange form of knowledge, most chillingly made actual at the end of James's story 'The Beast in the Jungle': 'This horror of waking – *this* was knowledge, knowledge under the breath of which the very tears in his eyes seemed to

---

[8] William Righter, *American Memory in Henry James*. Aldershot and Burlington: Ashgate, 2004, p. 160.

freeze.'[9] What this man has awoken to is an awareness of an entirely missed life, of sheer emptiness as dire completion. Nothing has happened to him, but it has happened three times, so to speak: throughout his life, while he waited for what he didn't have; on the one crucial occasion when he could have chosen otherwise; and now, when he receives his freezing knowledge of the void from which there is no return.

Densher takes Milly's letter, unopened, to Kate. They both know what is in it. Know? They guess. No, they know. They know Milly will have left him a lot of money, because she is, as they say, 'stupendous'. Kate burns the letter, still unopened; and because the novel has spent so many of its later pages in Densher's murky and self-deceiving consciousness, we may be rather surprised to find she thinks that the whole scheme a tremendous success, that everything has gone more or less as planned. 'We've not failed,' she says even before the letter comes. 'We've succeeded ... She won't have loved you for nothing ... And you won't have loved me' [462]. He will have loved her enough, in other words, to have passed, to the end, to Milly's end, as the person who didn't love Kate, that is, as the person who loved Kate so much that he could deny her in order to keep her. This, of course, is what he has not quite managed to do.

In fact, things have gone terribly wrong, and neither Kate nor Densher, lucid as they are, is quite able to see what a wreck they have made of their love. Kate has been clear throughout about their goal and the lies it would cost. She has paid the price in lies, and her moral comfort is that she

---

[9] Henry James, 'The Beast in the Jungle', in *Complete Tales*, ed. Leon Edel. London: Rupert Hart-Davis, 1964, p. 402.

really liked Milly and wanted her to be happy, and genuinely felt that Milly could have what she wanted while she, Kate, a little later, would also get what she wanted – even if both wanted the same thing. Densher's comfort has been that he hasn't lied, and there is a weird moral dimension in which his honour is his deepest weakness, the flaw that makes him unworthy of the ruthless Kate. He didn't deny their relation when he last spoke with Milly, because he didn't have to, because Milly didn't ask. 'She wanted from my own lips – so I saw it – the truth. But I was with her for twenty minutes, and she never asked me for it.' 'She never wanted the truth,' Kate says devastatingly. 'She wanted *you* ... You might have lied to her from pity, and she have seen you and felt you lie, and yet – since it was all for tenderness – she would have thanked you and blessed you and clung to you but the more' [458]. Remaining faithful to Kate, as he thinks, Densher has come close to betraying their scheme, and has failed of tenderness towards Milly into the bargain. All he kept faith with was his own literalist, prevaricating notion of honour.

Still, his honour is not simply to be dismissed, and he finally understands precisely why it is that Kate is wrong about the success of their scheme. His understanding hinges on what he does and does not know about Milly's letter, the one Kate threw into the fire. Of course, he and Kate knew it would name a bequest, and the later communication from a New York lawyer confirms that. But the fact is that if he betrayed Kate's passionate ruthlessness and lucidity by his prevarication, Kate took something precious away from him by burning the letter. It was hers to burn, he had given it to her. 'He had given poor Kate her freedom', we are told [503]. But since when was he able to say 'poor Kate', and why can he say it now? Because he is thinking that he will 'never,

never know what had been in Milly's letter'. He knows what it says, but not how Milly said it, and the thought of 'the turn she would have given her act' produces the image of an irrevocable loss, the forfeit of a revelation he will now never have, 'like the sacrifice of something sentient and throbbing, something that, for the spiritual ear, might have been audible as a faint far wail' [503]. Densher's understanding is complex and muffled, even distanced through the imagery that James lends him. But he has found his way to the idea of sacrifice, and what is wrong with the sacrifice of the innocent.

Densher offers to marry Kate without the money, or if they don't marry, to give the money to her. Kate accuses him of falling in love with Milly at their last interview, that is, falling in love with the future dead girl: 'She died for you then that you might understand her' [508]. And just as he couldn't tell Milly that he and Kate were not engaged, Densher cannot now tell Kate, when she asks him point blank, that he is not in love with Milly's memory. He is dismissive about the idea, but Kate insists. 'Don't speak of it as if you couldn't be. *I* could in your place' [509]. This is 'the knowledge of each other that they couldn't undo'. He can't love, perhaps never loved enough, the strength he thought he loved in Kate. She can't bear his lapse into guilt, which he has crystallized in the dead girl. Kate has, as she said earlier, taken trouble for him she 'never dreamed' she should take 'for any human creature' [393], and the creature has sought forgiveness and blessing in the very moral scheme she had grandly set aside. When worldly designs succeed, as Dorothea Krook suggests, their success redefines our scruple. With success Kate would have left her father's world far behind. She and Densher would have married, the memories of shady dealing would have faded and Milly would have been remembered as an immense benefactor. Densher wants to put away the bad memories by not taking the money, but his even thinking of doing this, let alone his doing it, undermines the whole scheme and turns it into a moral disaster. Now the very attempt to outride scruple seems not heroic but simply unconscionable, and it invites us to believe that for all her magnificence Kate was never going to get out of the land of disgrace, as Densher was never going to make any money.

IV

Robert Pippin, in an excellent recent book called *Henry James and Modern Moral Life*, summarizes these dilemmas starting from Densher's point of view. Pippin says that Densher can't take the money because he can't, in the end, act 'as if no great moral complication would shadow their life'. If this view is right, Kate must be in the wrong, and have always been in the wrong. She 'plausibly disagrees', Pippin says, because she sees that they can't retrospectively put themselves in the right. But were they in the wrong? 'Interestingly', says Pippin, it doesn't seem so to Kate.[10] We might ask, although Pippin doesn't, whether Kate's amorality is in any way defensible, and indeed whether it might not be a sort of morality. But with or without this question, what do we think has happened? Has Densher arrived late at the right morality, or is he just trapped in some blurred and generalized sense of guilt? The right morality, Pippin wants to argue, has something to do with Milly's 'entitlement' not to be treated in the way she was treated. There is always the possibility, Pippin continues, 'that such judgments are vestigial or sentimental or finally empty', but he doesn't think

[10] Robert Pippin, *Henry James and Modern Moral Life*. Cambridge: Cambridge University Press, 2000, pp. 1–3.

James believes they are, or always are. James is not a 'moral sceptic'. 'I don't think there is any question,' Pippin says, 'that James is treating Kate's attitude as wrong, and the interesting issue has been all along why he thinks that, what else he must be committed to in order to believe it.'[11]

I don't think there is any question that Pippin and I regard Kate's attitude as wrong, and James may well have felt the same. But the novel itself, with its extravagant moral subtlety and its exemplary moral discretion, makes some very strange suggestions, a few of which I have evoked more or less in passing. That honour may be a form of weakness. That ruthlessness may be a kind of probity, and in its clear-sightedness may even generate more tenderness than honour is likely to. That success and failure alter the moral dimensions of any worldly action. Could it be that the novel is a moral sceptic, even if James isn't? What does this novel know?

It's worth remembering that novels can be deeply pre-occupied with morality without offering any moralizing, and that they are under no obligation to endorse our views or anyone else's – indeed, we might think they are under some obligation not to do any endorsing at all. But this is not the same as asking what they know. *The Wings of the Dove* suggests, perhaps contrary to our expectation of a James novel, and contrary to many familiar readings of this one, that knowledge is very often fully available but entirely unwelcome. This is a little odd, given James's interest in perpetual enquiry and the difficulties of knowing, and his often remarked propensity for verbs of perceiving and descrying. Things are always 'seeming' and 'appearing' and 'as if', and Seymour Chatman has listed a host of

[11] Ibid., pp. 4, 177.

words and phrases of discovery in James's later work : 'see that', 'see how', 'make out', 'recognize', and of course 'learn' and 'know'.[12] It's true, as Ruth Yeazell has shown, that characters in James's late fiction regularly 'confront what in some part of themselves they have long since known', and that knowledge is for them 'both deeply desired and profoundly terrifying'.[13] But what I have in mind is something blunter, less delicately Jamesian. In *The Wings of the Dove* Kate's family has no wish to know what Lionel Croy has done. Milly doesn't want to know the name of her illness, and Susan Stringham doesn't either. Kate, having speculated about the same thing, decides that 'it's a matter in which I don't want knowledge', adding that Milly 'doesn't want one to want it' [284]. Densher doesn't want to know anything about the actual situation he has got himself into, and is capable of wonderfully hazy bits of argument such as the following: 'The single thing that was clear in complications was that, whatever happened, one was to behave like a gentleman – to which was added indeed the perhaps slightly less shining truth that complications might sometimes have their tedium beguiled by a study of the question of how a gentleman would behave' [367]. Neither Aunt Maud nor Susan Stringham is interested in the truth of the relationship between Densher and Kate. Densher and Kate burn Milly's letter without reading it, and although Kate reads the New York lawyer's letter and knows how much Milly has left to Densher, he hasn't read the letter and doesn't want to know. And finally there is the unundoable knowledge of each other

---

[12] Seymour Chatman, *The Later Style of Henry James*. Oxford: Blackwell, 1972, p. 19.
[13] Ruth Bernard Yeazell, *Language and Knowledge in the Late Novels of Henry James*. Chicago: University of Chicago Press, 1976, pp. 33, 54.

that Kate and Densher bury in each other's arms, or that he at least thinks they are burying there.

This all adds up, it seems to me, to a story not of epistemological uncertainty or moral relativity but of willed and systematic blindness. By looking closely at the question of knowledge in *The Wings of the Dove* we come to see how rarely people want it. When Kate says her father's disgrace is 'known – only ... not to us', she seems to anticipate Franz Kafka's famous remark to Max Brod. Kafka told Brod that he sometimes saw our world as one of God's bad moods, or bad days. 'So there would be no hope outside our world?' Brod asked. 'Plenty of hope,' Kafka said, smiling, 'for God – no end of hope – only not for us.'[14] But of course Kafka is talking about an unfortunate exclusion, a kind of privilege that God keeps to himself, while Kate is thinking of an anonymous public record that she and her family don't have to pay any attention to: they are not excluded, they are excluding. Just think of what can be known and isn't in *The Wings of the Dove*: disgrace, illness, dishonesty, love, charity and an identifiable large amount of money. This is a lot not to want to know, and it's a very varied list. As James's narrator says at one point, these characters inhabit a world 'from which the specified had been chased like a dangerous animal' [440]. Contemplating the sheer force of deliberate blindness in the book, we can return to the question of Kate's wrongdoing.

Whatever Kate is, she is not blind. Even in her not wanting knowledge of Milly's illness, she is lucid about Milly's preference, and about her own sheer distaste for the very idea of illness. 'I'm a brute about illness,' she says. 'I hate it' [285]. 'If you want things named,' she later tells

---

[14] Max Brod, *Franz Kafka: A Biography*. Translated by G. Humphreys Roberts and Richard Winston. New York: Da Capo Press, 1995, p. 75.

Densher, 'you must name them' [394]. This is just before she
makes him spell out their plot in all its greedy and ghoulish
detail: 'Since she's to die I'm to marry her?' But once he's out
of her presence, Densher is no great shakes at naming things,
rather an expert at dodging categories; and with or without
him Kate remorselessly calls things by their precise and proper
names. In this novel to name is to know, and to know you
know, and Kate is almost alone in doing this. Her only
companion is Milly, who names things, or some things,
when she can, and learns fast. She understands, for instance,
that Kate may be 'the least bit brutal', although she isn't
'brutally brutal – which Milly had hitherto benightedly supposed the only way' [171]. It's a tribute to her that she doesn't
like Kate any the less for this, and it is because they both try to
name things and to know things that they hit it off so well.

Kate isn't brutally brutal, and she isn't deceptively decep-
tive. She offers a paradoxical case of openness in a world of
hiding because her own lie is so clear and logically grounded.
It's hard not to feel that this quality in her is some kind of
virtue, even when she is manifestly engaged in swindling a
dying girl out of her money. James has crafted an exquisite
moral dilemma for us as well as for his characters, and we,
too, like Kate, find ourselves knowing more than we can say
('She knew more than she could have told you' [72] is
James's phrase), and even perhaps like the child Maisie,
perceiving more than we can translate. There is, I think,
no way of describing the morality of what is happening in
this novel without getting it wrong, and I've been doing it
for some time.[15] If we admire Kate for her clarity and her

---

[15] Sharon Cameron offers a subtle and troubling way around the dilemma
by suggesting that the 'allegory of good and evil' in the novel is under-
mined by an 'entirely unthematized counterallegory of thinking, which

courage, her wish to have what she can have, we seem to be endorsing what the least moralizing of critics, F. W. Dupee, calls 'traffic in the affections',[16] and most critics go a lot further. Dorothea Krook calls Kate's scheme diabolical and dreadful. I'm not much of a moralizer myself, but I have used the words greedy, ghoulish, shabby, disgrace and swindling. But to use any of these words and leave them standing is to have missed everything that matters about Kate, and to have misrepresented our own feelings about her and her actions.

Couldn't she be clear and brave and crooked at the same time? No. Because what we admire in her is her straightness. But she could be clear and brave and wrong. The question – Pippin's question and now ours – is how she is wrong, what exactly she is wrong about. I don't believe in Pippin's notion of Milly's 'entitlement' to certain forms of treatment, or rather her entitlement not to be treated in certain ways, but the answer to our question must centre on Milly. If it is all right to deceive a person into happiness, as Kate and Densher (and Aunt Maud and Susan Stringham) seek to do with Milly, if happiness is happiness, deceived or undeceived, then Kate's scheme is unconventional and indirect, but can't be substantively wrong. And surely it can be all right to deceive a person into happiness, and has been on many occasions, even when the happiness in question was not the primary aim of the scheme. Why not here? Because happiness is not the issue in Milly's case. Love and life are the issue, to have loved, to have lived. But an obstinate, practical

incapacitates traditional ways to understand it, and for which there is no comprehensible "other" level of significance'. That is, the novel unravels the very notion of thinking, about morality or anything else. *Thinking in Henry James.* Chicago: University of Chicago Press, 1989, p. 190.

[16] F. W. Dupee, 'Afterword', *The Wings of the Dove*. New York: Signet, 1964, p. 509.

doubt remains. Hasn't Milly finally loved and lived, even if in error about her dawdling suitor? Isn't it the discovery of the error that kills her, takes away her will to live, rather than the error itself? Wasn't the error working just as well as the truth would have? I know these sound like dastardly questions from any sound moral point of view, but that is what I am suggesting the novel does for us. It rattles not our morals but our sense of their reasonableness, and that is why we are in such a fix when we try to talk about the book.

I should like to say that everyone in this novel has too cheap an idea of Milly's desire for experience, that is, fails to see the depth and extent of her longing, and is too ready to give her just a little life and imagine she is happy with it. After all, as we might brutally say, she is dying, how much can she expect? Kate thinks Milly lacks the imagination of terror (by which, interestingly, she means the imagination of thrift and dependence on others, the things that terrify Kate), but Kate herself lacks the imagination of disinterested knowledge, the knowledge I suggested earlier was for James synonymous with life. When Milly is surprised by Susan Stringham on the edge of a mountain in Switzerland, 'looking down on the kingdoms of the earth', Susan realizes that Milly is not planning to renounce any of them. The question is, 'Was she choosing among them or did she want them all?' [135]. The biblical parallel is important, the reminiscence of the scene where Satan offers the kingdoms of the earth to Christ, but the novel also offers, in relation to this scene, several echoes [134, 137, 143, 282, 333] of one of the closing phrases of *Paradise Lost* ('The world was all before them') and there is nothing diabolical about Milly's refusal to renounce. She doesn't want to possess the kingdoms of the earth – she already possesses enough – she wants to know them. No one else in the novel understands this, and this shows a poverty of imagination on their part – on the part even of the most imaginative. But is this a moral failing? Does it justify all the ugly words we want to use?

Yet we continue to want to use the words, or many of us do. We want to say, with Dupee, that in Kate's case even 'infinite fascination and understanding'[17] can't lead to forgiveness, but I'm not sure that forgiveness even comes up as an impossibility. Morals are what they are, but the shifting world is also what it is. Roland Barthes contrasts knowledge itself, and not only morals, with life as it is lived. 'Knowledge is coarse, life is subtle, and literature matters to us because it corrects this distance.' I'm translating the French word '*science*' as knowledge, rather tendentiously, but it's clear that the English word science doesn't catch what's meant. '*La science est grossière, la vie est subtile, et c'est pour corriger cette distance que la littérature nous importe.*'[18] Let's say science here means organized knowledge, and in this context would mean organized ethical thought. Organized thought would be coarse and life would be subtle – a reversal of a familiar assumption. Barthes also writes of a fundamental failure of relation between language and reality, an '*inadéquation fondamentale du langage et du réel*'.[19] I think, too, of J. L. Austin's phrase about 'the innumerable and unforeseeable demands of the world upon language'.[20] We have words, as Austin shows, that help us to meet these demands, but we also have, like Maisie, perceptions we cannot translate into words. And if those perceptions come to us from a work of literature, we may find we cannot happily translate them into words others than those we have already been given.

---

[17] Dupee, 'Afterword', p. 509.   [18] Barthes, *Leçon*, p. 18.   [19] Ibid., p. 22.
[20] J. L. Austin, *Sense and Sensibilia*. Oxford: Oxford University Press, 1964, p. 73.

We do translate them, but we can't do it happily. Recognizing this fact, pausing over the untranslated perceptions, settling for coarseness when we have to, but remembering the subtlety we have just betrayed, is not moral relativism but a form of patience, a way of looking the world's complexity in the face. Of course, patience is not everything and time won't always wait for us. This also is part of what the novel knows. Henry James knows all this, too, of course, but I'm not sure it's the main thing he knows, and the novel knows it on every page.

CHAPTER 2

After such knowledge

I

In this chapter I'm going to trace out an argument about what it means to claim some forms of knowledge for literature and not others, and about what happens when we try to situate literature between the worlds of work and play. The journey is both long and accelerated, and it may help if I say something about its chief stages. I'm going to suggest, with the help of a number of critical and philosophical friends, most of them personally unknown to me:

— that literature may know a lot about us that we would rather it did not know;
— that it often, perhaps mostly, lets us off the hook by telling us that what it has on us is not real knowledge;
— that literature likes to say it is only playing at knowing things but that we shall do well not to be entirely taken in by this assertion, because although it often does play at knowing things, sometimes it's not playing;
— and finally that if literature is not always playing, we may need to take the thought one stage further and recognize situations where the play has become reality without our knowing it.

II

'Literature doesn't say it knows something,' Roland Barthes
once announced, 'but that it knows of something.' I don't think
the kinds of knowledge Barthes is evoking – the knowledge
that literature says it doesn't have and the knowledge it says it
does – are mysterious or unusual. They are ordinarily called,
respectively, direct knowledge and knowledge by acquaintance. A novel such as *Robinson Crusoe* displays many forms
of knowledge (*savoir*), Barthes says: historical, geographical,
social, technical, botanical, anthropological, and so on. But
literature doesn't fix or fetichize any of these knowledges,
'*elle n'en fixe, elle n'en fétichise aucun*'. So far there is no
particular difficulty in translating the French: '*la littérature ne
dit pas qu'elle sait quelque chose, mais qu'elle sait de quelque chose.*'

The place where things get tricky – that is, difficult to
translate and in my view deeply suggestive about the relations between literature and knowledge – is in the rest of
Barthes's sentence. He seems to rephrase the idiom 'to know
of' as 'to know about', but actually displaces it; and having
displaced it, elaborates on it, fills it with hints of unspoken
knowledge. Here is the full sentence, which begins with the
statement that the knowledge set in motion by literature is
never complete or final. '*D'autre part, le savoir qu'elle mobilise
n'est jamais ni entier ni dernier; la littérature ne dit pas qu'elle
sait quelque chose, mais qu'elle sait de quelque chose; ou mieux:
qu'elle en sait quelque chose – qu'elle en sait long sur les
hommes.*' ('The knowledge it marshals is, on the other
hand, never complete or final. Literature doesn't say it
knows something, but that it knows *of* something; or better,
that it knows *about* something – that it knows about men.')[1]

---

[1] Roland Barthes, *Leçon*. Paris: Seuil, 1978 pp. 18–19. Translated by
Richard Howard in *A Barthes Reader*, ed. Susan Sontag. London:
Jonathan Cape, 1982, p. 463.

Let's do this in slow motion. There is a difference, in French and in English, between knowing of and knowing about. Knowing of suggests mere acquaintance and knowing about could mean possessing substantial information. But there doesn't have to be much of a difference, and we do use the phrases as near-synonyms. The difference between *savoir de* and *en savoir* is only grammatical, involving an indirect object in the second instance, but of course Barthes's leaning on the syntax suggests there is more going on, and hints at something perhaps a little sinister in the second phrase: '*en savoir*' suggests a very knowing form of knowledge. Literature now seems to know of things in the way an intelligence agency might – if there were intelligence agencies that knew anything.

But it's Barthes's next move that really shifts the ground. '*La littérature ... dit ... qu'elle en sait quelque chose – qu'elle en sait long sur les hommes.*' ('literature ... says ... that it knows *about* something – that it knows about men.') About women, too, I take it, but 'men' is what the French says. '*En savoir long*' is certainly different from '*en savoir*', and it is shrewd of Richard Howard to drop the emphasis on quantity, since in English 'knowing about' can easily include the notion of knowing a great deal about. There is a strong flavour of gossip about Barthes's phrase, perhaps even of weariness, a hint of many stories that could be told, and will be told if we are not careful. Literature knows a lot; it knows too much. It knows more than it wants to know, perhaps; and almost certainly more than we want it to know. This is a long way from the apparent disavowal of knowledge with which the proposition started, and some considerable distance from simple knowledge by acquaintance.

It is in this context that Barthes makes the remark I quoted in the previous chapter: '*La science est grossière, la vie est subtile, et c'est pour corriger cette distance que la littérature nous importe.'* ('Organized or systematic knowledge is crude, life is subtle, and it is for the correction of this disparity that literature matters to us.')[2] The idea of correction, I take it, is a metaphor from the world of vision, and evokes the prescription lenses that may correct our sight, that is, bring it closer to a norm, or bring objects into focus. A more idiomatic translation would perhaps say 'corrects for this distance'. '*Science*' must include science among its meanings. But it can't here mean just the natural sciences, and it is clearly related, both etymologically and in the sequence of Barthes's thought, to the other word he is using for knowledge: '*savoir*'. Literature, he says a little earlier, '*fait tourner les savoirs*', makes our different bodies of knowledge circle or spin, or even, I would suggest, given the general spirit of Barthes's remarks, makes them dance. Later Barthes says that writing makes knowledge into a feast or a holiday: '*l'écriture fait du savoir une fête*'.[3]

But the metaphor of correction is our main focus here, at least initially. Knowledge is coarse and life is subtle, but literature is not offered to us as some kind of middle ground, like porridge at just the right temperature. It is neither knowledge nor life but it is both crude and subtle. It corrects for the distance in the sense of allowing us to live with the distance, which will mean both magnifying and shrinking things, and involve all kinds of pretences. In fact, the situation is even more complicated than Barthes suggests. Knowledge is not always crude, life is not always subtle, and knowledge and life are not always opposed or at a distance. In many of its physical and biological aspects, for

[2] *Leçon*, p. 18; *A Barthes Reader*, p. 463.
[3] *Leçon*, pp. 18, 20; *A Barthes Reader*, pp. 463, 464.

example, life on our planet is as organized as the strictest science could wish – that organization is precisely what several of our sciences study.

Nevertheless, much of life (persons, places, events) does not get turned into knowledge; and much knowledge is helpless when faced with the speed or unpredictability of life. We do need a space where knowledge is present but not working, like a doctor spending an afternoon at the cinema – not on call but still available if the terror or the pathos of the film should prove too much for someone. And where life is not present but well represented, alluded to or simulated, so that it will seem we can ask questions of its very vagaries. Both knowledge and life get a day off, so to speak; '*un jour de fête*', as in the title of Jacques Tati's film.

There are drawbacks to this picture. Is the day off really a day off, and should it be? Is literature no more than a holiday designed to make us more productive in the working year? There may be a serious underselling of literature in Barthes's celebration of its obliquity, but even so, his little allegory about literature and knowledge is full of precise and productive suggestions.

Barthes is saying that literature doesn't claim to know anything but it has the goods or the dope on us, could even perhaps – is this going too far? – blackmail us. It corrects for the distance between knowledge and life. It makes knowledge spin, perhaps makes it dance, perhaps makes it dizzy – this is itself a dizzying thought, but it makes sense in terms of correction, if knowledge on occasion has to be made dizzy to bring it closer to the dizziness of life. And literature not only gives knowledge a holiday, it makes knowledge into a holiday. Between the chance of blackmail and the chance of a vacation, we have plenty to be going on with.

III

It is no accident that – this is the phrase writers always use
when they are about to do something slippery with their
argument. Let me start again. It is not, I hope, merely a piece
of random free association on my part that brings together
Barthes's idea that literature makes knowledge into a holiday
and Ludwig Wittgenstein's image for the occasions when
philosophical problems arise: when language goes on holiday. The sentence appears in *Philosophical Investigations*.
'Denn die philosophischen Probleme entstehen, wenn die
Sprache *feiert*' (Wittgenstein's italics).[4] *Feiern* is the close
equivalent of *fêter*, and a *Feiertag* is a *jour de fête*. The double
sense is even clearer in these French and German words than
it is in the English holiday. A holiday is when you do
something, celebrate, commemorate, have a party; but
mainly, in ordinary practice, it's a day when you do nothing,
when you just don't go to work. So what happens when
knowledge and/or language takes a holiday? Is Barthes's
literature another name for Wittgenstein's philosophical
problems? And if this connection between Barthes and
Wittgenstein is not a piece of free association on my part,
what is it? Let me throw another famous philosophical
proposition into the mix, and then I'll try to answer these
questions. Here language is on holiday again, and literature
is also involved:

A performative utterance will, for example, be *in a peculiar way*
hollow or void if said by an actor on the stage, or if introduced in a
poem, or spoken in soliloquy. Language in such circumstances is in

[4] Ludwig Wittgenstein, *Philosophical Investigations*. Translated by G. E. M.
Anscombe. Oxford: Blackwell, 1967, p. 19.

special ways – intelligibly – used not seriously, but in ways *parasitic* upon its normal use – ways which fall under the doctrine of the *etiolations* of language.[5]

You will have recognized an important but intricately embarrassed sentence from J. L. Austin's *How To Do Things With Words*. 'In a peculiar way', 'parasitic', 'etiolations' are all marked by Austin's cautious italics, and the whole passage, of course, has always made literary people unhappy.

IV

A pause for definitions, although I hope the argument will move along a little even during the pause. I'm not using the words literature or knowledge in any special or technical ways, but even in their ordinary senses they have quite precise if capacious meanings, and it will be worth briefly saying what they are.

Literature used to mean, and in certain restricted areas still means, written material of any kind, material that needs to be read – as literate continues to mean being able to read. Since the end of the eighteenth century, in Europe at least, it has meant, in Raymond Williams's words, 'well-written books of an imaginative or creative kind'.[6] Pierre Macherey, in *A quoi pense la littérature*, situates the rise of this notion of literature between 1760 and 1800, or, to give proper names, between Lessing's essays on aesthetics and Mme de Staël's *On Literature*. But then literature in this sense has a strong

[5] J. L. Austin, *How To Do Things With Words*. Edited by J. O. Urmson. New York: Oxford University Press, 1965, p. 22.

[6] Raymond Williams, *Keywords*. London: Fontana, 1983, p. 186.

continuity with what, from the Greeks all the way to the European eighteenth century, used to be called poetry, and although all of my chief examples are late enough to be called literature I do want us to think about whatever is evoked by poetry in the old sense and by literature in its modern sense. That is: representations or imitations of life as it might be and perhaps is; imaginary people doing real things; real people doing imaginary things; more rarely, imaginary people doing imaginary things; and more rarely still – I shall return to this instance in my last chapter – real people doing real things, but not the things they actually did. The term 'fiction' has come to cover much of the same ground, but I want to save an exploration of it for later, because it carries a rather different philosophical freight, and because it seems, on the face of it, fully to accept a condition (not-fact, not-reality, not-truth) that 'literature' and 'poetry' never quite settle for.

'Imaginative or creative' are Williams's honorific words for literature, or rather his words for registering the way literature has come to be honoured – and perhaps marginalized. But traditional accounts of literature and poetry often include, among their extravagant praises, some more dubious terms. 'Representation' and 'mimesis' are fairly neutral, but 'imitation' already opens a little door to worry, and 'feigning' and 'counterfeiting', also popular words, open a wider door. Sidney glosses Aristotle's word mimesis as 'a representing, counterfeiting, or figuring forth – to speak metaphorically, a speaking picture'. A little later Sidney tells us that the poet cannot lie. 'He nothing affirmeth, and therefore never lieth ... And ... though he recount things not true, yet because he telleth them not for true, he lieth not.' But the notion of counterfeiting cannot be shaken off so easily. There is always a joke about imposture or lying lurking in the idea of poetry and literature, and Sidney himself, although unequivocal in his defence of poetry, enjoys the joke greatly. Even Plato was a poet, he suggests, in spite of the philosopher's strictures on imitation, because 'all standeth upon dialogues, wherein he feigneth many honest burgesses of Athens to speak of such matters, that, if they had been set on the rack, they would never have confessed them'.[7] Of course, the joke is not always a joke. For George Eliot it was a qualm about the very idea of imaginative literature, for Henry James it was the subject of a range of intricate short stories, and for Thomas Mann it was the basis of a whole oeuvre, from the earliest version of *Felix Krull the Confidence Man* to the latest.

Even Hesiod's Muses were not above a little teasing of humans on this subject. 'We know how to tell many falsehoods that seem real,' they said, 'but we also know how to speak truth when we wish to.'[8] This is a wonderful definition of literature and poetry, in the aspects we are exploring, and expertly names the criss-crossing dilemma which is at the heart of this book. Except that it's not a dilemma. It's just what literature looks like when you put questions about knowledge to it. Listening to those Muses, we might well get all kinds of things wrong. We might look to them for knowledge when they were just telling us convincing lies. But equally we might ignore them when they were telling us the truth – just because we know they are capable of lying. We could get a few things right, too, and we might need, once again, the interpretative patience I have already

[7] Philip Sidney, *A Defence of Poetry*. Edited by Jan van Dorsten. Oxford: Oxford University Press, 1966, pp. 25, 52–53, 19.
[8] Hesiod, *Theogony*. Translated by Norman O. Brown. Indianapolis: Bobbs–Merrill, 1953, p. 53. See also Christopher Gill and T. P. Wiseman, eds. *Lies and Fiction in the Ancient World*. Exeter: University of Exeter Press, 1993, passim.

invoked. We could make an attempt to sort out the lies and the truths, and we might even think a clear perception of any given mixture of lies and truths was a very precious form of knowledge. 'There is truth in lies too,' a character says in an old American movie, 'if you get enough of them.'[9]

The idea that poetry is more philosophical than history, as Aristotle said it was, includes the possibility that history might be less accommodating than poetry. This is the ground of a wonderful sequence in the second part of *Don Quixote*, where Quixote learns that a book has been written about him – the first part of Cervantes's novel – and that it does not entirely represent him as he wishes to be represented. I'm going to linger a moment here, because the twists of the argument are revealing, and it isn't all that often that Aristotle serves as the trigger for an inspired comedy routine.

The book about Don Quixote has been written, we learn, by one Cide Hamete Benengeli, described as a moor and a sage, '*moro y sabio*', and the book has been translated by someone Cervantes met in the market in Toledo. What has been published, under Cervantes's name, in more than twelve thousand copies, is the transcription of this translation. You can already see why someone interested in direct knowledge claims might be getting nervous. Quixote is very pleased with the news. 'One of the things', he says, 'that must give the greatest contentment to a virtuous and eminent man is to see, while he is still alive, his good name printed and published in the languages of different peoples.'[10] He gets a

---

[9] *The Ox-Bow Incident*, 1943, directed by William Wellman and written by Lamar Trotti.

[10] Miguel de Cervantes, *Don Quixote*. Madrid: Austral, 1998, p. 602. Translated by Edith Grossman. New York: HarperCollins, 2003, p. 475.

little worried, though, when he is informed that Cide Hamete has told all. The participants in the following discussion are Quixote himself, Sancho Panza, and Sansón Carrasco, a student, who has read the book in question or at least knows a lot about it, '*en sait long*'.

'The wise man,' responded Sansón, 'left nothing in the inkwell; he says everything and takes note of everything, even the capering that our good Sancho did in the blanket.'

'In the blanket I wasn't capering,' responded Sancho, 'but I was in the air, and more than I would have liked.'

'It seems to me', said Don Quixote, 'there is no human history in the world that does not have its ups and downs, especially those that deal with chivalry; they cannot be filled with nothing but successful exploits.'

'Even so,' responded the bachelor, 'some people who have read the history say they would have been pleased if its authors had forgotten about some of the infinite beatings given to Señor Don Quixote in various encounters.'

'That's where the truth of the history comes in,' said Sancho.

'They could also have kept quiet about them for the sake of fairness,' said Don Quixote, 'because the actions that do not change or alter the truth of the history do not need to be written if they belittle the hero. By my faith, Aeneas was not as pious as Virgil depicts him, or Ulysses as prudent as Homer describes him.'

'That is true,' replied Sansón, 'but it is one thing to write as a poet and another to write as a historian: the poet can recount or sing about things not as they were, but as they should have been, and the historian must write about them not as they should have been but as they were, without adding or subtracting anything from the truth.'[11]

In this context, to say poetry is more philosophical than history is only to say history is more scrupulous than poetry.

[11] *Don Quixote*, p. 603; *Don Quixote* (English) pp. 475–476.

What's dizzying, of course, is that these are fictional characters talking about the truth and falsehood of purely fictional events.

Aristotle himself was not always as transparent on this subject as many of his readers have thought, and he can sound a little like Cervantes (or even Borges) if you hold him up to a certain light. Here's how the argument in the *Poetics* goes. 'It is not the function of the poet to relate what has happened, but what may happen – what is possible according to the law of probability or necessity.' This is not a matter of verbal form. Even writing in verse, Herodotus would still have been a historian. 'Poetry ... is a more philosophical and higher thing than history: for poetry tends to express the universal, history the particular.' And Aristotle repeats the point about 'the law of probability or necessity'. A little later he says that the poet 'should be a maker of plots rather than verses, since he is a poet because he imitates, and what he imitates are actions'.[12] 'Plots rather than verses' is a point of emphasis rather than exclusion, a reminder that although many poets use verse, it's not verse that makes them poets. No great difficulty so far, I think, except the one lurking in the idea of probability and necessity as alternatives. They are very different grounds of appeal, and there is a lot of space between them.

The fun starts when Aristotle explains why tragic poets like to use the names of actual people in their plays. There is, of course, no reason why an actual person should not represent the universal, but that is not what Aristotle says. His line is that the tragic poets keep the actual names because 'what is possible is credible: what has not happened we do not at once

[12] Aristotle, *Poetics*. Translated by S. H. Butcher. New York: Hill and Wang, 1961, pp. 68–69.

feel sure to be possible, but what has happened is manifestly possible: otherwise it would not have happened'.[13] So a poem, by definition an imitation of what may happen, can also be about what has happened, or more precisely, can claim that some things may happen because they already have. And then Aristotle makes one more dizzying move. A poet will be 'none the less a poet' if he takes 'a historical subject', 'for there is no reason why some events that have actually happened should not conform to the law of the probable and possible'.[14] 'Possible' here seems to have again the meaning of 'logically or physically possible' as at the beginning of the passage, rather than its tautological meaning of 'possible because undeniable'. This is a little untidy, certainly wrecks the neat distinction between poetry and history, and I wonder whether 'otherwise it would not have happened' may not be a deadpan joke. But the very untidiness is revealing, and part of Aristotle's fidelity to his slippery subject.

Poetry, and later literature, show us what may happen but hasn't; they use historical data all the time; and history itself can be shaped as a drama or an epic. There is no problem with the poems themselves, since successful works create their own conditions of belief and acceptance. The trick is to

[13] Ibid., p. 69.
[14] Ibid., p. 69. Other translations of this interesting sentence: 'for nothing prevents some actual events from being probable or possible'. (*On Poetry and Style*, translated by C. M. Grube. Indianapolis: Bobbs-Merrill, 1958, p. 19); 'for there is nothing to prevent some of the things that have happened from being the sort of things that may happen according to probability, i.e. that are possible' (*Poetics*, translated by Richard Janko. Indianapolis: Hackett, 1987, p. 13); 'there is nothing to prevent some actual events being probable as well as possible' (*Poetics*, translated by Stephen Halliwell. Cambridge: Harvard University Press, 1995, pp. 61–63).

understand how they do this, and what rules we might devise for these relations. We know that the law of probability or necessity needs to be respected, and we believe it is respected in all proven poetic cases. But the argument is circular. We are convinced by what we find convincing, and call this conviction the effect of a law: these are the kinds of things we think happen. Probabilities are not events in the world, they are the expression of a view of the world, and so we don't always know ('we do not at once feel sure') whether any given new instance meets our law or breaks it. That's when we start saying the possible is what has already happened, and vast theoretical gulfs open up on all sides. Are historical events probable and necessary, like poetic actions but with the addition of actuality? Hardly, since history, for Aristotle as for anyone else, is full of the improbable and the accidental, and sometimes has only its actuality going for it. So poetry is more philosophical than history not only because it expresses the universal, but because it recognizes important laws of meaning and coherence. But then we seem to be saying not that poetry relates what may happen but that it arranges happenings according to a dream of order, and the suspicion of lying comes up again. Aristotle's sentences suddenly seem to be full of what they are not saying. 'There is no reason why' some historical events should not be probable, but there is no reason why they should, apparently, and perhaps not many of them will be. This is how we can preserve our distinction between poetry and history. Poetry leaves history to its own improbable devices, but the probable itself becomes more and more unlikely, a desperate fantasy rather than a noble model. I realize this reading is a little perverse, even upside down, since obviously Aristotle knows and insists on the difference between ordinary lying and 'the art of telling lies skilfully', alias poetry.[15] But I'm interested in the lurking sense of untruth, the suspicion of fixing that cannot be shaken off, because it is so clearly a part of the continuing life of literature. If a poem couldn't be untrue, there would be no chance of its telling us the truth either.

We can say that the worry about lying doesn't have to arise when we read or think about literature, and very often doesn't. When it doesn't, there is really no question about literature and knowledge, or rather the question is already settled: literature affords us a special kind of knowledge, quite different from everyday knowledge, and not subject to its queries and verifications. We don't ask, as Dorothy Walsh puts it, 'Whether life ... does or does not stain the white radiance of eternity', and reading a novel that begins 'All happy families are alike', Walsh says, 'Probably few, if any, readers will be likely to pause over this and ask themselves: Is it so?'[16] I think Walsh is wrong about the second example, which I shall return to in a while, but the general point is clear. What I want to suggest is that the worry about lying always could arise, and often has, to the immense enrichment of literature; and that although there were always many ways of dealing with the worry, something drastic happened to the whole set of preoccupations in the later nineteenth century and after. Very roughly, the defenders of poetry defected, or more precisely, offered defences of poetry that were virtually indistinguishable from attacks.[17]

[15] Aristotle, *Poetics*, p. 109. For an excellent discussion of this issue, see Andrew Ford, *The Origins of Criticism*. Princeton: Princeton University Press, 2002, p. 231 and passim.
[16] Dorothy Walsh, *Literature and Knowledge*. Middletown: Wesleyan University Press, 1969, p. 47.
[17] Cf Paul Fry, *A Defense of Poetry*. Stanford: Stanford University Press, 1995, p. 3. 'By conceding truth to science (which had since taken over the role of philosophy in the quarrel), Arnold and I. A. Richards

I'm not enough of a historian to tell this story properly and in detail – it is a good story – and it is the aftermath of the story that forms my real subject. But obviously there is no aftermath without a math, and I can very quickly evoke a literary and critical scene you will instantly recognize. It is a place where a distinguished poet says, with whatever surrounding complexities, that the poetry does not matter;[18] where another distinguished poet, even if one also given to irony, says that poetry makes nothing happen.[19] Another modern poet says that a poem should not mean but be.[20] A famous critic tells us that 'the bulk of poetry consists of statements which only the very foolish would think of attempting to verify',[21] and whole sets of academic disciplines are cowed by the example of the natural sciences. Literature departments get so baffled by the need for quantitative reporting of what they are doing that they forget the name of their practice, and think of themselves as failing to find what they are not even looking for: knowledge in the hard, cumulative sense. I quote Stefan Collini's eloquent reminder: '"Knowledge" is too easily thought of as accumulated stock, as something that doesn't need to be discovered again … But "understanding" underlines that it's a human activity, and so is inseparable from the people who do it.'[22]

in their several defences of poetry gave back all the territory Shelley had gained.'

[18] T. S. Eliot, 'East Coker', in *The Complete Poems and Plays*. New York: Harcourt, Brace & World, 1971, p. 125.

[19] W. H. Auden, 'In Memory of W. B. Yeats', in *Collected Poems*. London: Faber & Faber, 1991, p. 248.

[20] Archibald MacLeish, 'Ars poetica', in *Collected Poems*. Boston: Houghton Mifflin, 1962, p. 51.

[21] I. A. Richards, *Principles of Literary Criticism*. New York: Harcourt, Brace & World, 1961, p. 272.

[22] Stefan Collini, *English Pasts*. Oxford: Oxford University Press, 1999, p. 237.

John Guillory wants scholars in the humanities to claim knowledge rather than understanding, although he, like Collini, refuses the idea of knowledge as simple accumulation. Guillory published a long and brilliant article on the Sokal hoax, far too intricate to summarize here, and interesting about all kinds of things other than the (rather dull) hoax itself.[23] Both Collini and Guillory are thinking about the interpretation of literature rather than literature itself, but there is a real continuity of question: poems and studies of poems deal in understanding, and we may want to say that they deal in knowledge. Guillory says that 'It has been notoriously difficult to give an account of the knowledge produced by interpretation that would not immediately invite invidious comparison with the sciences.' With the natural sciences, that is, but the claims of the social sciences already wait in the wings. 'The division of the disciplines into sciences and humanities has been triumphantly reconceived as the distinction between *knowledge* and the *critique of knowledge*' (Guillory's italics). To put this bluntly: they (the scientists) have the knowledge, and we (in the humanities) do the critique. They practise doubt that arrives at (provisional) certainty, we just practice infinite doubt, and get better and better at it. No wonder no one wants to give us any money. Scholars in the humanities have failed, Guillory argues 'to define and defend the knowledge claims of criticism'. And again: 'It may seem merely trivial now to claim

[23] In 1966 the physicist Alan Sokal published in the journal *Social Text* an article called 'Transgressing the Boundaries: Towards a Transformative Hermeneutics of Quantum Gravity'. No one seems to have thought this was a hoax until Sokal said it was, and much discussion followed in the press, offering on the one hand some rather predictable attacks on the abstruseness of cultural theory and on the other some rather casual defences of the delights of generalized scepticism.

for interpretation the status of knowledge. But the history of the disciplines has shown us that this is not a trivial claim at all.'[24]

It is easy to claim the status of knowledge for the historical study of literature, as of anything else. But Guillory's point specifically concerns criticism and interpretation. The argument of this book is that literature characteristically offers something harder – in the sense of the 'hard' sciences – than understanding and something softer than what we often imagine knowledge to be. The obliquity of literature is an important part of this offering, and makes direct claims of any kind seem a little crude. Still, there is no harm in speaking of knowledge, and we certainly shouldn't back off from such a claim when it needs to be made. But we could also look at the offering without rushing to give it a single name: sometimes we need to see round a name as well as with it or through it.

I have crossed from a definition of literature into an account of a claim for knowledge. But what about the definition of knowledge? In the previous chapter I looked at several kinds of knowledge, and several working senses of what knowledge is. But there are other questions we need to ask. Knowledge as opposed to what? Or as distinguished from what? There is an immense philosophical literature (in the older sense of the word) on this topic, although much of the discussion circles around intuitions about what the word means in ordinary usage. This issue turns out to be extraordinarily hard to settle, and some people have thought it couldn't be settled, or that we really don't know anything.

---

[24] John Guillory, 'The Sokal Affair and the History of Criticism', *Critical Inquiry* vol. 28, no. 2, Winter 2002, pp. 498, 505, 507, 508.

We just talk as if we did. Peter Unger, in a book called *Ignorance*, suggests that the thesis of radical scepticism – 'that no one ever *knows* anything about anything' – is not only famously difficult to refute, but might be difficult to refute because it's true.[25] Edward Craig says that this can't be the end of the story and that we must know a few things, even if not the ones we think we know. The word knowledge, Craig says, is not like the word witch. 'There is a very natural – though somewhat pathological – explanation of the fact that the word acquired such a meaning as not to apply to any of the many persons to whom it was applied, and was applied to them nevertheless.' We can't bracket or historicize the word knowledge in this way, because we still need it, and need it all the time. That is, we keep thinking it applies to something. 'There seems to be no known language', Craig remarks, 'in which sentences using "know" do not find a comfortable and colloquial equivalent.'[26] So remaining as comfortable and colloquial as possible, let's say that by knowledge we mean knowledge as opposed to opinion or belief, and knowledge as distinguished from awareness or experience. What, then, will it mean to say that literature makes knowledge into a holiday, *'fait du savoir une fête'*? It will mean the construction of a defence of poetry which reaches back beyond the modern defections, and much resembles many old defences; and yet also remains marked by those defections, and seems to give an awful lot away.

[25] Peter Unger, *Ignorance*. Oxford: Oxford University Press, 2002, p. 1 and passim.
[26] Edward Craig, *Knowledge and the State of Nature*. Oxford: Clarendon Press, 1990, pp. 70–71, 2.

V

My other questions, you will remember, were these. Is Barthes's literature another name for Wittgenstein's philosophical problems? And if the connection I am making between Barthes and Wittgenstein is not a piece of free association on my part, what is it? The answer to the first question is no. What Barthes means by literature and what Wittgenstein means by philosophical problems are not the same thing, but they do flourish in the same space, and this fact surely is interesting. The answer to the second question is that the very words literature and philosophy and holiday, once they are put together, become part of an old and ongoing discussion about work and play and whatever alternatives there are to either. It is an accident, if you like, that Barthes and Wittgenstein should settle on the same metaphor. But the reach of the metaphor, once chosen, is historically determined, the coordinates are already in place. Barthes and Wittgenstein, whatever their reasons for going there, have stepped into the same room.

Of course, they have different reasons. Barthes wishes to subtract literature from the world of power, metonymically represented by the implied world of work. He also wants, contra Foucault, to dissociate knowledge from power, and he seeks to do this by placing knowledge, or some forms of knowledge, on the side of play. He calls literature a 'salutory trickery', a '*tricherie salutaire*', which allows us to 'understand speech outside the bounds of power' ('*entendre la langue hors-pouvoir*').[27] I think Barthes does manage to break down the simple identity of power and knowledge, but I don't think he manages to keep all hints of power out of

[27] Barthes, *Leçon*, p. 16; *A Barthes Reader*, p. 462.

literature, even in its playful relation to knowledge. That is the whole point of the little allegory as I read it. '*En savoir long sur les hommes*', 'to know a lot about people', is to have something on them, something you could hold against them. My metaphor of blackmail may be too violent, but it makes this kind of relation visible. We can give the same thought a benevolent turn, and find the promise of such knowledge enlightening, even if still uncomfortable. I don't find it implausible to imagine that literature has this kind of power over us: we often see in it what we would rather not know about ourselves.

When Wittgenstein says philosophical problems arise when language goes on holiday, he means that words make sense when they are working but may get up to all sorts of things in their leisure hours, and that philosophy has spent too much time with them on their days off. The philosophers have been working, so to speak, while language was on holiday, and this mismatch has been the source of most, if not all our troubles. Wittgenstein has been puzzling over what he calls our tendency to 'make sublime [*sublimieren*] the logic of our language'. I don't think he means sublimate, and G. E. M. Anscombe gives us 'sublime' as a verb. He means a tendency to shift our logic too readily into the realm of the sublime, or to make it occult. Philosophers have thought that naming, for instance, is 'an occult process', a 'strange [*seltsam*] connexion of a word with an object'. And Wittgenstein imagines a philosopher trying to 'bring out *the* relation between name and thing by staring at an object in front of him and repeating a name ... innumerable times'.[28] This is a philosopher who clearly needs a holiday.

---

[28] Wittgenstein, *Philosophical Investigations*, pp. 18, 19.

Although one is recommending it and the other is resisting it, Barthes and Wittgenstein meet up in the idea of holiday. But we can go further than this. Knowledge is not entirely on holiday for Barthes – there are all kinds of ways in which knowledge is working in literature, even in Barthes's disengaged sense – and language is not entirely on holiday for Wittgenstein, since it is leading philosophers astray. The metaphor of holiday successfully resists or recommends the idea of work, but the idea of a real holiday disappears in the process.

It is at this point that the quotation from Austin can help us. 'A performative utterance will, for example, be *in a peculiar way* hollow or void if said by an actor on the stage, or if introduced in a poem ...'[29] Is language on holiday here? We may want to say it is relieved of quite a few of its real-life duties. But we might also want to say it is working harder than ever. If we said this, though, we would need to redefine work, retaining Austin's notion of 'normal use' for certain functions of language, but insisting that in literature language is not etiolated but hyperactive. But let's pause for a moment over the studied vagueness of Austin's own language. 'In a peculiar way'; 'in special ways'; 'intelligibly'; 'not seriously': this is how a performative utterance will work in a play or a poem, Austin says. In real life, if I say the right words at a marriage ceremony, I am married – assuming that all the proper legal arrangements are in place, and that I am not a bigamist. If I say the same words in a play, I am also married – as a character in the play, I am as married as anyone can ever need to be. It doesn't seem right to say I can't get married because I'm only imaginary – what kind of discrimination is that? Of course, as an actor I don't

[29] Austin, *How To Do Things With Words*, p. 22.

get married by saying these words – or at least not by saying them on stage, at this place and this time. 'In a peculiar way', 'in special ways', 'intelligibly', 'not seriously' all turn out to mean, in the old idiom, poetically or feigning. To quote Sidney again: 'The poet never maketh any circles about your imagination, to conjure you to believe for true what he writes.'[30] Ah, but he does. We can scarcely tell the poet from the magician. He wants us to believe and not believe, and the extraordinary thing is how good we are at performing this double act, virtually without thinking, and without the least strain.

VI

Literature makes knowledge into a holiday – and then makes that holiday into something else, creates a new zone between work and play – because it renders all knowledge hypothetical, even the hardest and most familiar knowledge, like that of the layout of city streets and the bitter effects of poverty. Literature frames knowledge with visible or invisible sentences saying, 'If I were to say this' and 'now that these possibilities have been laid out'. We read, to return to the example I borrowed from Dorothy Walsh, 'All happy families are alike; each unhappy family is unhappy in its own way.'[31] And we say: They are if you say so, and as long as the families are fictional, and stay within this novel. If we open another novel – Nabokov's *Ada*, for instance – we find an opening sentence that says, with deliberate clumsiness, exactly the opposite: 'All happy families are more or less dissimilar; all

---

[30] Sidney, *A Defence of Poetry*, pp. 52–53.
[31] Leo Tolstoy, *Anna Karenina*. Translated by Richard Pevear and Larissa Volkhonsky. London: Penguin, 2000, p. 1.

unhappy ones are more or less alike.'[32] And we say: They are if you say so. Literature is like logic in this sense, and has its logic: we grant to each work its declared premise or premises.

And yet. This is precisely where the metaphor of the holiday breaks down, or runs out of steam. More: literature couldn't correct for the distance between life and knowledge if the metaphor didn't finally break down. Literature does not simply refresh us so that we can return to nonliterary work, it helps us to do the work of deciding what we do and do not know. Literature, to repeat, renders all knowledge hypothetical, it pretends to affirm when it is not affirming. But every pretend affirmation could also be the real thing, crying out for testing. The proposition that all happy families are alike is a premise we can grant, and no doubt need to grant, but it's not just a literary premise, or doesn't have to be. It's also a matter of some importance, although undoubtedly rather hard to settle, whether the proposition is true, and it is certainly worth arguing about – in this sense *Ada* is an argument with *Anna Karenina*. And sometimes the pretend affirmations don't look like pretences at all. 'You must change your life.'[33] 'One must have a mind of winter.'[34] 'Lose something every day.'[35] I shall come back in a later chapter to a whole set of instances of this kind. Perhaps it would be foolish to attempt to verify these statements or test these instructions, but only because verifying and testing seem such grudging short-term projects. As Angela Leighton nicely says, commenting on an early

[32] Vladimir Nabokov, *Ada*. London: Penguin, 1971, p. 9.
[33] Rainer Maria Rilke, 'Archaic Torso of Apollo', in *Selected Poetry*, trans. Stephen Mitchell. New York: Vintage, 1989, p. 61.
[34] Wallace Stevens, 'The Snow Man', in *Selected Poems*. New York: Vintage, 1959, p. 23.
[35] Elizabeth Bishop, 'One Art', in *The Complete Poems*. New York: Farrar, Straus and Giroux, 1979, p. 178.

work by Heather McHugh, if wanting poetry to be about something is criticism's shortsightedness, wanting it not to be about anything may be poetry's. 'Conversations between the two, however ill-tempered and high-flown, are still those of fellow travellers.'[36] Propositions in poems may in the end be more speculative than they look but they may also represent unequivocal advice, urgently given and perhaps urgently needed. This is precisely what Hesiod's Muses said so long ago: that they knew how to tell convincing lies, and also how to tell the truth when they wished. There is no safe place here: no literalist's haven where fact is always fact; and no paradise of metaphor, where fiction has no truck at all with the harsh and shifting world.

VII

For a long time I used to want to write a parody of Auden's poem 'Musée des Beaux Arts' which would begin 'About suffering they were always wrong, / The old bastards . . . ' It wasn't that I disliked Auden's poem or disagreed with its drift – on the contrary, the poem has always been one of my touchstones for understanding many things about the world. I wanted to underscore (to simplify) what I take to be one of the central meanings of the poem itself, and to suggest that wondering about whether the Old Masters could possibly be wrong is one of the things the poem asks us to do.

Here is the poem.

> About suffering they were never wrong,
> The Old Masters: how well they understood

[36] Angela Leighton, 'Elegies of Form in Bishop, Plath, Stevenson'. *Proceedings of the British Academy*, vol. 121, 2002.

Its human position; how it takes place
While someone else is eating or opening a window or
just walking dully along;
How, when the aged are reverently, passionately
waiting
For the miraculous birth, there always must be
Children who did not especially want it to happen,
skating
On a pond at the edge of the wood . . .
They never forgot
That even the dreadful martyrdom must run its course
Anyhow in a corner, some untidy spot
Where the dogs go on with their doggy life and the
torturer's horse
Scratches its innocent behind on a tree.

In Brueghel's *Icarus*, for instance: how everything turns away
Quite leisurely from the disaster; the ploughman may
Have heard the splash, the forsaken cry,
But for him it was not an important failure; the sun
shone
As it had to on the white legs disappearing into the
green
Water; and the expensive delicate ship that must have
seen
Something amazing, a boy falling out of the sky,
Had somewhere to get to and sailed calmly on.[37]

The old people are waiting, the children skate, the dogs go
on with their doggy life. The dogs are ordinariness personified,
entirely indifferent to martyrdoms, dreadful or otherwise. The
torturer's horse is a little different. Innocent itself, of course
(well, its behind is innocent), but pretty close to the gruesome
action. Of course the horse doesn't care about its master's job,

---

[37] Auden, 'Musée des Beaux Arts', in *Collected Poems*, p. 179.

and there is something wonderfully Brueghelesque about its just scratching its behind on a tree. This is Old Masterly wisdom, not about human indifference but about the stubborn attractions of ordinary life. It's good that the torturer's horse should be innocent, that its behind, needing to be scratched, can get scratched; that there is a tree handy, that the horse knows what to do for its relief. But: it is a torturer's horse, and no one else's, and we are not going to get this fact out of our heads.

'In Brueghel's *Icarus*, for instance'. We note the mock casualness with which Auden produces the title of the painting, reminding us that he has in mind not just any old Musée but the one with this work in it, the one in Brussels. But then what is Icarus an instance of? Of suffering? Well, of flight and skill and failure; of 'disaster', and 'how everything turns away' from it. The failure is touching, even in the Brueghel, so that the story doesn't seem to be about arrogance and hubris, but about falling and vanishing, human ambition wrecked and fatal, and not even noticed. How many Icaruses, the implication is, do we fail to see each day?

What Auden's poem adds up to is not a claim that the Old Masters were never wrong about suffering and its human position. That's a hyperbole, that's the poetic part, the convincing lie, if you like. It's that they were not wrong enough, not as wrong as we would like them to be, even need them to be – that's the truth the Muses will tell us, if we are ready to listen. Or to translate into Barthes's terms, the claim about the Old Masters offers crude knowledge, and the details of the poem imitate subtle life. The correction for distance occurs through our managing not to slight or ignore either partner to the relation.

The Old Masters could be wrong, like anyone else, but what about the person who can't help being right? In closing this chapter I want to turn to Borges, and to what I shall call the parable of the truthful imposter. 'Who can boast,' we read in 'The Babylon Lottery', 'of being a mere imposter?' (*'Además, quién podrá jactarse de ser un mero impostor?'*)[38] The suggestion is not that we can't boast about being imposters if we feel like it, and not that we can't, on occasion, actually be imposters, only that we can't be *sure* of being imposters, even when we think we are. We can't, that is, entirely rely on our falsehoods, we can't guarantee that truth will not catch up with us, or catch us out. This proposition is the mirror image of the notion of literature I was evoking earlier: that form of feigning or counterfeiting which is never entirely safe from the charge of simply lying. Here is a form of lying which is never entirely safe from the charge of telling the truth.

The story appears in the first section of *Ficciones*, first published in 1941. The narrator, far from Babylon, and waiting for a boat to take him who knows where, recounts the history of the lottery for us. It was at first the kind of lottery we are all familiar with. You buy a ticket, or in this case a bone or parchment marker, there is a draw, you win or don't win a certain sum of money. A scheme without 'moral value', the narrator says, and the Babylonians soon moved on to something more sophisticated. They placed a few penalties among the prizes, so that you could be fined as well as just rewarded or unrewarded. When a certain number of players refused to pay their fines, they were prosecuted, and put in gaol. After a while, the lottery results no longer mentioned the amounts of the fine, only the number of days to be spent in gaol. 'It constituted the first appearance in the lottery of non-pecuniary elements' [69/67].

---

[38] Jorge Luis Borges, *Ficciones*. Madrid: Alianza, 1997, p. 76. Translated by Anthony Kerrigan. New York: Grove Press, 1962, p. 71. Further quotations are taken from these editions and are indicated in brackets on the page, Spanish text first.

The next move was to remove altogether the major pecuniary element: the purchase of the ticket or marker. The lottery now became 'secret, free of charge, and open to all', and its operations became so complex that the Lottery Company became the major civil power, took on '*la suma del poder público*' [70–71/68]. Every sixty nights there was a new draw, which determined the players' lots until the next draw. A single event – the murder in a tavern of A, the mysterious apotheosis of B – might be the end product of thirty or forty separate draws. Finally it was decided that the lottery should intervene at all stages, large and small, of Babylonian life, and that everything, the flight of a bird or the addition of a grain of sand to a beach, should be subject to a draw, or the rule of chance.

The lottery in its more advanced stages is defined as 'an interpolation of chance into the order of the world' ('*una interpolación del azar en el orden del mundo*') [72/69], but there are two kinds of chance, it turns out. There is the Company's chance, the infinite play of chances set in motion and controlled by the Company; and there is mere, pre-Company chance, which the Company cannot allow. The Company thus abolishes chance in the ordinary sense, since it subsumes everything into its planned operations; and it also intensifies chance by introducing it into areas of life where other causalities, time, age, ambition, desire, mechanics, conspiracy and so on, ordinarily rule. Chance is everywhere, but nothing is left to chance.

In a further mischievous turn, Borges's narrator tells us that 'Our historians . . . have invented for a method of correcting chance', ('*nuestros historiadores . . . han inventado un método para corregir el azar*') [75/71], and this is where the parable of the truthful imposter appears. By introducing mistakes, exaggerations, fictions into the history of the Company, the individual historian makes a small return to ordinary causality, performs a sequence of actions not governed by the drawing of a number: 'No book is ever published without some variant in each copy. Scribes take a secret oath to omit, interpolate, vary. Indirect lying is also practiced' [75/71 – the last sentence is missing in the English version].

Note the extraordinary turn here. The errors and slips and inconsistencies that we would usually take as the signs of chance at work in a world principally governed by (successfully) organized human intentions, become the tiny, enfeebled marks of human intention in a world thoroughly dominated by chance. But Borges – this is Borges after all – reserves one more turn for us. How do we know our errors are errors? Who can boast of being a mere imposter?

> The Company, with divine modesty, eludes all publicity. Its agents, as is only natural, are secret. The orders which it is continually sending out do not differ from those lavishly issued by imposters. Besides, who can ever boast of being a mere imposter? The inebriate who improvises an absurd mandate, the dreamer who suddenly awakes to choke the woman who lies at his side to death, do they not both, perhaps, carry out a secret decision by the Company? [75–76/71]

The truthful imposter is the figure who wrecks Austin's picture of the parasitic performative utterance and the etiolations of language. He is the man who thinks he is a bigamist but turns out to have been divorced without his knowledge, and so finds himself acting in good faith against his own will and awareness. He thinks he is in a play or poem, in this case of his own devising, but he's not. Or he is the actor in a play who steps offstage to find himself caught up in a story much resembling the one he has just left. Or he is the author who invents a world only to find reality has beaten him to it, as happened to Philip Roth when, in *Our Gang*, he made up a wildly satirical version of the language and behaviour of

Richard Nixon's cabinet only to discover, after Watergate, that his fantasies were the most mundane realism. A sensible person will say: But these are exceptional, fanciful instances. These are not the normal relations of truth and lies. You wouldn't turn to Borges for an assertion of the reality principle. And what's more, with the exception of the Roth case, these are just literary instances, faint possibilities.

But no one is saying the instances are normal, and it is precisely to the point that they arise in literature. Borges is asking a question and offering a speculation. His question is, 'Who can boast of being a mere imposter?' and his speculation is that persons who are apparently free agents may in fact be carrying out unawares the decisions of a secret organization. This has been known to happen, and in many different regions of life, from espionage to smuggling and psychoanalysis. What matters, and what literature knows in this context, is that the practical answer to these questions is not the only answer, even practically. In an averaged-out, 'normal' world, it will take a lot of divorced bigamists to change the protocols of meaning. Every new instance can be treated as an exception until the pile just gets too high. Only if most of the supposed bigamists turn out to have been divorced without their knowledge shall we have to regard this condition as the new norm. In literature it takes only one truthful imposter to put the very idea of the 'normal' to flight. What literature knows is how vulnerable we are to what Henry James called 'operative irony': 'It implies and projects the possible other case.'[39] Resisting the thought of this other case may seem like mere sanity, and it often is; but resisting it all the time is going to look like an expression of fear.

[39] Henry James, *The Art of the Novel*. New York: Charles Scribner's Sons, 1962, p. 222.

CHAPTER 3

Kafka and the Third Reich

I

In the year 1914 Franz Kafka wrote most of what we have of *The Trial*, abandoned in January 1915; and he wrote 'In the Penal Colony', the most historically freighted, and most clairvoyant, of all his stories. Clairvoyant? Is this a casual metaphor or a serious claim to foreknowledge? It is a metaphor, but not a casual one. The knowledge is only knowledge, but none the less impressive and frightening for that.

In the first part of this chapter I look at the ways in which Kafka's characters seek to domesticate surprise, to refuse the extraordinariness of the extraordinary. Of course, they shouldn't be trying to do this. No one should have to live through the unlivable, or be driven to think the manifestly unthinkable. But history has shown us that moral imperatives, like logic itself in Kafka's view, are 'no doubt unshakable, but ... can't withstand a person who wants to live'.[1] The second part of the chapter explores what we might call the moral engineering of the extraordinary, the way people

---

[1] Franz Kafka, *Der Proceß*. Frankfurt: Fischer, 1993, p. 244. *The Trial*, Translated by Breon Mitchell. New York: Schocken Books, 1998, p. 231. Further quotations are taken from these editions and are indicated in brackets on the page, German text first.

can represent (and have represented and are representing) an appalling atrocity as, in their case, a special exercise of virtue. 'I have learned one thing,' the speaker says in Geoffrey Hill's poem 'Ovid in the Third Reich'. 'Not to look down/So much upon the damned.'[2] The suggestion, I take it, is that the damned are not as far from us as we like to think they are. This doesn't mean that they, and perhaps we, are not damned.

In his book on Hitler J. P. Stern writes of Kafka's 'prophetic imagination', and his 'surprising anticipations' of what was to come in Europe.[3] And even earlier, in the *Cambridge Review* in 1964, Stern had asked the question that underlies this chapter, and that has indeed never left my mind since I first read it in this formulation. Stern is reviewing a book about Milena Jesenská, Kafka's friend, who died in the Ravensbrück concentration camp. Jesenská 'understood', Stern says, 'that all those doubts and apprehensions that haunted [Kafka] and imperilled almost every one of his friendships were at the same time the materials from which his work was built', and 'in the last years of her life she lived out some of the terrors which his stories had intimated and described: experiencing in her own person, what she had read nearly two decades earlier'. For these reasons, Stern says, the book about her, *Kafkas Freundin Milena*, by Margarete Buber-Neumann, 'throws a powerful light on one of the major questions of our time: the question, that is, of what connection there may be between the world of Franz Kafka and the world of Ravensbrück'.[4]

---

[2] Geoffrey Hill, 'Ovid in the Third Reich', in *Collected Poems*. Harmondsworth: Penguin, 1985, p. 61.

[3] J. P. Stern, *Hitler: The Führer and the People*. London: Fontana, 1984, p. 49.

[4] J. P. Stern, 'The World of Ravensbrück', *Cambridge Review*, 6 June 1964.

Stern's phrasing is cautious, and allows for the possibility that there may not be a connection. It allows some space also for those who wish neither to make too firm or causal a link nor to see no link at all. Stern's later work eloquently shows that there are several bridges to be built, but rather fragile ones, and each needs treating with great care. We need to remember, too, that in Stern's question both Kafka and Ravensbrück have become figures of speech, parts that stand for apparently widely separated wholes – at the widest point of separation, perhaps, for literature itself and the racial policies of the Third Reich. What do we think when literature seems to know about a particular horror well before it happens?

In his Hitler book Stern shows Kafka making the connection himself, not as a prophecy but as an analogy. In his unsent *Letter to His Father*, Kafka writes:

> Your self-confidence was so immense that you had no need to be consistent at all and yet never ceased to be in the right ... You could, for instance, run down the Czechs, and then the Germans, and then the Jews – not only selectively but wholesale, in every respect – until nobody was left but yourself. You assumed for me that mysteriousness which belongs to all tyrants whose right is founded not in thought but in their persons.[5]

Stern juxtaposes this passage with what he called 'the turgid diction' of the following claim in *Mein Kampf*: 'one man must step forward in order ... to form granite principles from the wavering world of the imaginings of the broad masses ... The general right to such an activity is founded

---

[5] Franz Kafka, 'Brief an den Vater', in *Hochzeitsvorbereitungen auf dem Lande*. Frankfurt: Fischer, 1991, p. 14. English translation from Stern, *Hitler*, pp. 48–49.

in necessity, the personal right in success.' In both cases, in Stern's gloss, 'a single man's vision is elevated to a law valid for all men, private arbitrariness to a system of political rules'. But then, Stern adds, Kafka 'has not a word of warning or of advice on how to resist the solipsistic evil he so clearly descries. Something of his bemused, suicidal passivity, too, belongs to Hitler's world.'[6]

There are three elements here, and only together – perhaps not even then – do they add up to a 'surprising anticipation'. There is a political thought on Kafka's part: that a tyrant founds his right in his person. There is an analogy: the father's brutal capriciousness, his 'mysteriousness' is like that of the tyrannical ruler, the family is like the despotically run state, and the children, especially the son, are like the bewildered people of such a state. And there is an attitude to tyranny, the 'bemused, suicidal passivity'. The investigation of this last condition is certainly Kafka's special domain, but the sense of foreknowledge rests on something else, something still missing from this equation: Kafka's fiction itself. What Kafka appears to have foreseen, what he shows in extraordinary ingenious detail in his stories and parables and novels, is not only tyranny and arbitrary rule, but the precise movements of the mind by which people seek to make such a state intelligible to themselves – the brilliant, desperate ways in which they try to think intelligibly about the completely unintelligible.

Stern's insistence on passivity is important in this context, and a troubling feature of his whole argument about what was happening in the Third Reich. But actually the condition is more complex than passivity, and we can take Stern's argument even further than he does, and indeed perhaps

[6] Stern, *Hitler*, p. 49.

not quite in the same direction. Josef K in *The Trial*, Stern suggests, struggles against his arbitrary arrest but also finds in it a form of personal distinction, 'as if his "arrest" amounted to some strange validation'. This is 'the moment', Stern says, 'when the desperate victim behaves as if what held him captive was something other, something more than, the tormentor's might masquerading as right'. There is a form of shame, he says, which is 'the shame, it seems ultimately, not of being in the wrong, but of being alone and weak, or rather of being in the wrong because [one] is alone and weak'. The 'insinuation that the exterminator is not wholly in the wrong', Stern says, 'is the secret belief of the age of Kafka and Hitler'.[7] Now they share an age. How much stronger could the connection be?

To understand this insinuation is not to blame the victim – although it's clear that the thought could be turned that way. It is to understand something of the tormentor's more than material power, and more important, to understand something of the desperation of a mind that cannot believe in its own entire innocence – as what mind can? Passivity is not complicity here because it is not, as I am suggesting, passivity at all, but a strenuous attempt to deny the full dimensions of the monstrosity which has taken over the world, to rein it back into some form of reason. What Kafka's fiction knows is how and why people do this. What it doesn't know, what I at least didn't see it as knowing until I read Primo Levi, is that the very monstrosity of the persecutions and murders of the Reich was a feature of their power over the minds of the victims. This couldn't be happening, people thought. Even as it was happening, it couldn't be happening. And when it had happened, it couldn't have happened.

---

[7] Ibid., pp. 115, 116, 137.

This is part of what Levi calls the Reich's 'war against memory', but the war began while the memories were still in the making or unmaking. Levi quotes an address of the SS to their prisoners: 'However this war may end, we have won the war against you; none of you will be left to bear witness, but even if someone were to survive, the world will not believe him.'[8] 'The implausibility of their actions', Theodor Adorno says of the Nazis in *Minima Moralia*, 'made it easy to disbelieve what nobody ... wanted to believe.'[9] Kafka's fiction doesn't show us any easy disbelief, but it does show us, again and again, what it is like to be faced with the unthinkable, and to fail to think it.

A man, young or of indeterminate age, in any case not old, finds himself suddenly in a situation of radical uncertainty. He is a passenger on a ship which has just docked in a foreign country; he arrives at night in a sleeping, snow-covered village; he has just had a conversation with a ghost; he has woken up to find himself transformed into a gigantic insect; early one morning he is arrested. I am describing situations that occur, respectively, in *Amerika*, *The Castle*, a story called 'Unhappiness', another story called 'The Metamorphosis' and *The Trial*, and of course there are many such moments in Kafka. I'm going to look in a little more detail at the last two.

All these situations are Kafkaesque, of course, and not only because Franz Kafka set them up. But what truly belongs to Kafka, I think, and perhaps does not belong to our idea of the Kafkaesque, is not the initial dislocation or nightmare but what happens next. Or rather, what doesn't

[8] Primo Levi, *The Drowned and the Saved*. Translated by Raymond Rosenthal. New York: Vintage, 1989, pp. 31, 11.
[9] T. W. Adorno, *Minima Moralia*. Frankfurt: Suhrkamp, 1951, p. 138. Translated by E. F. N. Jephcott. London: Verso, 1978, p. 108.

happen next. The man, in each case, fails to hang on to the sense of strangeness the situation seems to call for. He treats it as if it were almost normal, or as if it could soon be made quite normal. As if he could be at home where no one could be at home. He denies or hides his ignorance or shock, anxiously asserts his control of what seems manifestly uncontrollable, even if his control is only mental, a matter of seeing round the corners of all possible arguments.

Was a simple refusal of the situation possible? Probably not, but there is some distance between an impossible refusal and a would-be canny embrace. What Kafka is offering us, I think, is the image not only of an ordinary world invaded by the extraordinary, but also of an extraordinary world which can't be seen as such. An image, that is, of the desperate reconstruction of ordinariness, of ordinariness as a last resort. As if the notion of the ordinary cannot be abandoned, whatever happens to it. Hannah Arendt's phrase about the banality of evil comes to mind, at least as an analogue. Kafka would be showing us the attempted domestication of horror, an understandable, even touching method of trying to live with what we can't manage, but which has the effect of making it all the more unmanageable. 'Today, at this very moment,' Primo Levi says, 'as I sit writing at a table, I myself am not convinced that these things happened.'[10]

The opening sentence of 'The Metamorphosis' is one of the most famous in world literature. 'When Gregor Samsa awoke one morning from troubled dreams, he found himself transformed in his bed into a monstrous insect.'[11] Gregor is

---

[10]   Primo Levi, *If This is a Man*, later published as *Survival in Auschwitz*. Translated by Stuart Woolf. New York: Simon & Schuster, 1996, p. 103.

[11]   Franz Kafka, 'The Metamorphosis', in *Sämtliche Erzählungen*. Frankfurt: Fischer, 1970, p. 56. *Metamorphosis and Other Stories*. Translated by Malcolm Pasley. London: Penguin, 2000, p. 76. Further quotations are

lying on his hard beetle's back, he can see his many tiny legs waving in the air. He wonders what has happened to him and assures himself that this is not a dream. He looks around his room and out of the window, is saddened by the rainy weather, wonders if he should go back to sleep, but can't manage to roll over on to his side. Then he thinks about his job as a commercial traveller. 'On the move, day in, day out' [56/77]. He recalls his worry about train connections, the irregular, bad food, the casual human contact. Above all, about having to get up so early. He has already missed the five o'clock train. Perhaps he should call in sick? When Gregor's father and sister ask him why he's still in bed, he says he'll be up soon. His voice is a little altered – it is later described by someone from Gregor's office as the voice of an animal – but at this stage Gregor is 'not in the slightest doubt' that the difference is just an early sign of a coming cold, one of the occupational diseases of the commercial traveller [59/79].

The story continues with its eerie, elaborate development, through Gregor's near-adjustment to his condition, to a final family showdown and Gregor's dusty death. Here I want only to insist on the uncanny mixture of lurid change and selective continuity which Kafka is laying out for us. Gregor has an insect's body but a human consciousness – more precisely a human consciousness modified, over time, by its habitation of an insect's body. His tastes in food change, and he finds he enjoys crawling over the walls and ceiling of his room. On the other hand, although he can't make himself understood, he continues to understand perfectly all the human conversations he hears and overhears. I'm not

taken from these editions and are indicated in brackets on the page, German text first.

suggesting that the horror consists in Gregor's preservation of human consciousness rather than his transformation into an insect, only that the precisely orchestrated patchiness of the transformation is what makes this story – which Kafka once called 'an exceptionally sickening story'[12] – so memorable. Its most distressing and haunting moment perhaps occurs not when Gregor crawls away to die, which is bad enough, but when he momentarily rejoices in the removal of the furniture from his room, which will leave him much more crawling space on the walls and the floor. His mother is upset at the alteration, and thinks everything should be left as it is, so that 'when Gregor returns to us he'll find everything unchanged' [80/103]. Hearing her say this, Gregor is aghast at the speed – he has been living as an insect for two months – with which he has forgotten 'his human past', and he crawls up an empty wall to press himself against what remains of his old furnishings, namely a picture of a fur-coated lady clipped from an illustrated magazine and framed behind glass. 'This picture at least, which Gregor now covered completely, was definitely not going to be removed by anybody' [82/105]. Gregor has become not only an insect, but a desperate insect, and worse still, an insect with a failing or forfeited human memory, the model of a failed adaptation to the unthinkable, but one which came distressingly close to success.

The same pattern of desperation and its attempted management appears in *The Trial*, which begins 'Someone must have slandered Joseph K, for one morning, without having done anything wrong he was arrested' [7/3]. 'Arrested' here is being used in an eerie, almost nonsensical way. Kafka uses two words for the situation: '*verhaftet*' and '*gefangen*'. The

[12] Cited by Paul Raabe in the notes to *Sämtliche Erzählungen*, p. 397.

first literally means held and the second literally means caught; neither really allows for the possibility of going on with your life as usual, as K is allowed to. K himself uses the term 'accused', '*angeklagt*', which plays an important part in the book later. But in this first chapter the other two terms dominate, and invite us to imagine a strictly unnameable condition: an arrest which does not detain, an imprisonment which is neither literal nor metaphorical and not even virtual but something like a change of moral lighting, a stark alteration of an unaltered life.

When K is summoned for a first interrogation, he is given a day and an address but no time. He decides more or less arbitrarily – because that's when courts begin their work on weekdays – to go at nine. We are then told again that he wants to get there at nine, 'although he had not even been required to appear at any specified time' [43/38]. He gets lost in an unfamiliar neighbourhood, is considerably delayed, and on arrival is told that he is late – not just late in general terms, but exactly an hour and five minutes late, late by the timetable that only he is supposed to know.

This is not to say that the court exists only in K's mind – the very idea rests on a distinction between mind and world which is not tenable in Kafka's world, and not always tenable in ours. The eerie telepathy about the time of the session suggests not that K has imagined the court, in the sense of making it up, but that the court has thoroughly imagined K, in the sense of knowing how his mind works. The court is real, we might say, a formal institution as firm and brutal as anything else in this fictional territory. But it has many faces and forms and the ones we see are the ones intended for K – more precisely, the ones attuned to K, tailored for him, the way any indictment, however impersonally framed, is full of the personality of the accused. Unless of course the whole

indictment names the wrong person. Even K can't quite
think that, and this, too, is part of the belief that the tormentor – the tormentor who is to turn into an exterminator –
cannot be wholly in the wrong.

One of the guards who have come to arrest K explains
how things work. 'Before ordering such an arrest the higher
authorities who employ us inform themselves in great detail
about the person they're arresting and the grounds for the
arrest. There's been no mistake. After all, our department, as
far as I know, and I know only the lowest level, doesn't seek
out guilt among the general population, but, as the law states,
is attracted by guilt, and has to send us guards out. That's the
law. What mistake could there be?' K says that he doesn't
know that law, but the guard simply replies, 'All the worse
for you' [12–13/8–9]. This looks like, and is, a travesty of
the law as we imagine it in modern civil society; slightly less
of a travesty of how the law often works even in such a
society. It is a perfect picture of how the law works in
totalitarian societies. 'Why, do you think we would sum-
mons someone who hasn't done anything?', as Stern remarks
in his Hitler book, 'is not a quotation from *The Trial*, but the
reply of a Gestapo official to a question by a Jewish woman
who is about to be delivered to her death.'[13]

But a law attracted by a guilt it does not seek out is also a
perfect picture of many other laws, mostly invisible and
unwritten ones – the law of conscience as well as the law
of superstition, for example, the law of the Christian and
Jewish God as well as the law of self-tormenting mania. We
are not asked here, as many readers of Kafka have felt they
were, and as Orson Welles manifestly thought he was for his
film version of *The Trial*, to exclude what we know of

[13] Stern, *Hitler*, p. 114.

spiritual imperatives in order to sustain a critique of a giant bureaucracy. But nor are we asked, as many other readers of Kafka have felt, notably Max Brod, to forget what we know about bureaucracy in order to keep afloat in the spiritual dimension. We are asked only to see that the same language can be used for a monstrous (and historically familiar) breach of civil law and for the ordinary relations of God and the troubled soul. We are more expert in both regions than we think; a lot less expert in working out what it means that they can share a language.

Characters in Kafka (and not only in Kafka) often behave as if the world is either just what it is or an elaborate conspiracy against them, an implementation of their bad dreams. Kafka himself seems to have thought these were pretty much the alternatives, but what his most poised and perfected work suggests is that both self and world are mixed packages, bundles of fiction and fact, truth and lies. They are, we might say, both conspiracies but conspiracies necessarily engaged with each other, and what we call reality is the result of their clash or tangle, nothing else. Conspiracy is probably too violent a metaphor, but I'm trying to dramatize the sense, very strong in Kafka but also in a number of other modern writers, of reality as an intricate set-up rather than a collection of objects or truths – solid enough, but held together by its articulations, not by the sheer gravity of its matter. 'The world is everything that is the case', Wittgenstein writes.[14] I'm not sure how much scepticism hides in this assertive sentence but it is clear that 'is the case' is not the same as 'exists' or 'is true'. Wittgenstein's later phrase for this state of affairs, also a perfectly idiomatic phrase in everyday German, is '*wie es sich*

---

[14] Ludwig Wittgenstein, *Tractatus Logico-Philosophicus*. Translated by C. K. Ogden. London: Routledge, 1981, p. 31.

verhält, literally what relations obtain, translated by G. E. M. Anscombe as 'the facts'.[15] The point in this context is that there are no facts in the German idiom, only connections or proportions. Kafka uses the same idiom in just the same way, and it is striking that when Gregor Samsa thinks of getting back to some kind of noninsect reality he thinks of *'die Wiederkehr der wirklichen und selbstverständlichen Verhältnisse'* ('the return of the real and self-evident relations') [60/80], translated by Willa and Edwin Muir as the 'real and normal condition'[16] and by Malcolm Pasley as 'normal, unquestionable reality'. The world is everything that is self-evident, a set of self-evident relations. Or rather the real and the self-evident go together, confirm each other. A world wouldn't be real if it wasn't self-evident.

Self-evident is not the most idiomatic translation here, but the underlying implication is interesting. *Selbstverständlich* literally means self-intelligible, intelligible without further elaboration, and more generally means taken for granted, going without saying. In conversation you can use it to mean 'Of course', or 'Obviously'. What is to return for Gregor is a world to which you say, 'Of course'. Or don't even have to say it. The full context here is telling. Gregor is lying on his back, trying to be calm, breathing lightly. He is still near the beginning of his transformation, and he's thinking of getting up and taking the next train to work. Normality, he seems to think, will come back if he waits. He is wrong, but only because his insect life is a new reality, what is now the case, not because his old life wasn't real or the new one is a fantasy. This, I think, is what the word *selbstverständlich* helps us to see. The real and

<hr>

[15] Ludwig Wittgenstein, *Philosophical Investigations*. Translated by G. E. M. Anslombe. Oxford: Blackwell, 1967, p. 37.

[16] Franz Kafka, 'The Metamorphosis'. Translated by Willa and Edwin Muir in *The Complete Stories*. New York: Schocken Books, 1971, p. 93.

the ordinary, wherever and however they crop up, are only
partly a matter of understanding; more a matter of habit, of not
needing to understand.

II

Kafka's fiction repeatedly displays the disappearance of the
ordinary, the longing for the ordinary, and the failure of the
ordinary to return, and 'In the Penal Colony' is no exception.
But this story also shows us something else: not the desperate
turns of the victim's mind but the crazed dream of justice
which preoccupies a tormentor. I don't believe the construc-
tors of Ravensbrück were driven by any sort of dream of
justice, but many gaolers and exterminators were and are.
'In the Penal Colony' knows a lot about us, as Roland
Barthes would say. It is a picture of a place we must hope
never to enter – I leave it to you to decide how close we are
to it – a place where we are building our own version of
Ravensbrück and telling ourselves it is all right.

A traveller visits a French penal colony in the tropics and
is shown 'a peculiar kind of apparatus', an execution machine
which not only puts prisoners to death but inscribes on their
bodies the text of the law they have broken. In the case that is
about to be concluded, the words to be written are 'Honour
thy superiors!' The prisoner can't speak French, nor can the
soldier who is guarding him. The traveller asks the officer in
charge of the proceedings if the prisoner knows his sentence.
The officer says no, and adds, 'There would be no point
in announcing it to him. He gets to know it in the flesh.'[17]
A vast gulf of assumptions opens up – how could a body read a

---

[17] Franz Kafka, 'In der Strafkolonie', in *Sämtliche Erzählungen*, pp. 100, 104;
Metamorphosis and Other Stories, pp. 127, 131–132. Further quotations are

text through the locations of its wounds, in any language, let alone a language its owner doesn't know? – but no one pays any attention to it. The traveller asks, 'But at least he knows that sentence has been passed on him?' 'Nor that either,' the officer says, smiling. So the prisoner has no way of knowing whether his defence was effective. What defence? The officer explains that in this colony an accusation of guilt is enough. 'The principle on which I base my decisions is this: guilt is always beyond question' [104/132]. This man, for instance, was reported by a captain for sleeping on duty and for not taking kindly to being woken up by the lash of a whip across his face. 'If I had first summoned the man and interrogated him,' the officer says, 'it would only have led to confusion. He would have lied; if I had succeeded in refuting these lies he would have replaced them with fresh lies, and so forth.' The traveller reminds himself that he is in a penal colony and 'that special measures were necessary here, and that military procedures had to be adhered to throughout' [105/133]. But we are already deep in Kafka's universe of altered logic and displaced emphasis. Why is this violation of judicial process more extraordinary than the presence of a machine which tortures condemned men by writing on their flesh? Why is the officer smiling?

A striking feature of the story is the tone of ordinary reasonableness in which what seem to be entirely unreasonable, indeed inhuman arrangements are discussed – we have only to phrase things this way to see the 'prophetic' in Kafka's work. The traveller, for instance, feels 'some stirring of interest in the apparatus', as if it were a curiosity rather than a horror [102/130]. The officer describes in cool

taken from these editions and are indicated in brackets on the page, German text first.

detail the three parts of the machine with their 'popular'
('*volkstümlich*') names [101/129]. The condemned man lies
on something called the bed, another part called the designer
(literally the one who draws, '*der Zeichner*') receives instructions and formulates the text, and finally the harrow, an
elaborate arrangement of moving needles, writes on the
body for twelve hours. The officer mentions the bloody
mess of the operation as the 'only drawback' of the machine,
and complains about a noisy cogwheel, and the difficulty in
getting spare parts. The harrow is repeatedly said to be at
'work' on the body – the officer, in his way, clearly believes
that '*Arbeit macht frei* '.

Less luridly, but more eerily, the officer perfectly understands all the obvious arguments against his cruel system.
'You are conditioned by European ways of thought,' he says
to the traveller, 'perhaps you object on principle to capital
punishment in general and to this mechanical kind of execution in particular.' The traveller might feel like saying, 'We
have a different kind of judicial process', or, 'In our country
the accused is granted a hearing before he is sentenced', or
'We only used torture in the Middle Ages.' The officer then
makes an astonishing move. He says that these statements 'are
as true as they seem to you self-evident', but they have
nothing to do with what he is doing [112–113/142]. How
could they not? How could his sense of the standards of
what we think of as the civilized world not affect his own
assumptions? Because his whole mode of thought is dedicated
to other principles; grisly, harsh, but perfectly coherent and
passionately pursued. Certainly he is not just arguing for the
need for special discipline in a penal colony. He believes, as
the rest of the story makes clear, in the beauty and bodily
immediacy of a form of punishment no longer imaginable in
liberal (or even illiberal) modern societies. And as I have

suggested, in the particular detail of its inscriptions, unintelligible even as a form of punishment. At one point the officer seems disposed to plead for his death machine as 'the most humane and most worthy of humanity' [113/143], but this is only a possible argument he imputes to the traveller, and his main brief is quite different. He likes the mechanical intricacy of the machine itself, and the formality of the inscription, as well as the stern order the whole system represents.

The traveller thinks 'the injustice of the procedure and the inhumanity of the execution' are 'beyond all doubt' [109/138], but he listens carefully to the officer's accounts of the ceremonies in their heyday, and the anxious reader is half-afraid the traveller will be won over, especially when the officer evokes the 'transfiguration' of the condemned man at 'the sixth hour':

Enlightenment dawns on the dullest. It begins around the eyes. From there it spreads out. A spectacle that might tempt one to lay oneself down under the harrow beside him. Nothing further happens, the man simply begins to decipher the script ... How we all drank in the transfigured look on the tortured face, how we bathed our cheeks in the glow of this justice, finally achieved and soon fading! [108/137 and 111–112/141]

The word rendered here as script is '*Schrift*', often used elsewhere in Kafka, and often translated as scripture. The body, the officer is claiming, has read the text in a way the mind couldn't, justice itself has become flesh; albeit mortal, tortured flesh, in extremities of pain and on the edge of death. 'What's a mere guilty human life?' is the implied rhetorical question. A modest price for such an illumination, a lesson to us all, which even the victim enjoys before he dies.

The traveller, far too late for the comfort of most readers, finally makes himself clear. 'I am an opponent of this procedure,' he says to the officer, although he admits to being touched by the officer's 'sincere conviction' even in the realm of error [116/146]. And here comes what I find to be the most insidiously disturbing moment in this infinitely troubling story. The officer, who knows that the new Commandant and his followers have no time for him, finds it hard to believe that this sympathetic-seeming traveller is not on his side – because, we presume, he finds it hard to believe that anyone who is willing to hear the whole story won't be convinced by it. 'It did not look as if the officer had been listening. "So the procedure hasn't convinced you?" he murmured, smiling as an old man smiles at the nonsense of a child and pursues his own real thoughts behind that smile' [117/146].

There are lots of smiles like this in Kafka, but this one is particularly haunting. I can't help feeling we are looking at a strange, curiously human, if not humane, version of Adolf Eichmann; an Eichmann who is not a zombie or a robot. The officer knows what foreigners are likely to feel about his ghastly machine and the whole penal system, he knows what the new Commandant thinks, and he can't really be surprised at having failed to convince the traveller. He isn't surprised, but he is, weirdly, amused; amused at the traveller's failure to understand the elegance, coherence and justice of the procedure he has so carefully described; amused therefore at this further instance of the world's misunderstanding of what matters; and amused at the sheer loneliness of his own position, the isolating irony of being the sole surviving practitioner of what seems to him an ideal form of justice.

The officer decides to act on this irony. He releases the condemned man and sets about putting himself in his place. He alters the instructions for the writing machinery – the sentence now to be written on the body is: 'Be Just!' He smiles again, undresses and folds his uniform with great care, although this care sits a little oddly with the fact that he then abruptly throws each piece of clothing into the pit reserved for the body. He breaks his sword, and stands naked, ready for the law whose time, he says, has come. The traveller's behaviour is also a little strange here. He bites his lip and says nothing, although he can obviously see what is going to happen. In a few lines of indirect speech, we are told that if the whole procedure to which the officer was so attached was about to be abolished, then the officer was behaving entirely correctly. 'The voyager would have acted no differently in his place' [119/149]. The traveller seems to be applying some code of military honour, the one where the truant officer is given a revolver and expected to blow his brains out, perhaps; or the one where the masterless samurai falls on his sword. But Kafka's discreet dislocation of tone and substance means that this recognizable, even conventional notion seems mildly crazy. Would we feel it was quite right, entirely in order, if one of the last of the operators of the Holy Inquisition were to put himself on the rack? I find I am so troubled by the traveller's sympathy for the officer, and by Kafka's meticulous attention to the officer's smile, that I risk underrating the traveller's action in opposing the procedure. Kafka tells us that the man is 'fundamentally honourable and without fear' [116/146], and his firm words to the officer effectively trigger the end of a whole penal world, the officer's self-immolation and the disassembly of the machine. There is something more than 'bemused, suicidal passivity' here, and perhaps Kafka is telling us that speaking out does count, even if it comes late and can't shake off the odour of compromise.[18]

---

[18] I am grateful to Martin Davies for making this point so clearly in conversation.

The officer's devotion to the machine turns into a weird intimacy with it. 'It had been clear enough earlier that he understood the machine well, but now it was almost staggering to see how he handled it and how it obeyed him. He had only to stretch out a hand towards the harrow for it to raise and lower itself several times, until it reached the right position to receive him; he merely gripped the edge of the bed, and it began at once to vibrate ... ' [119/150]. When the officer is settled on the bed, he can't reach the crank to start the machine, but he doesn't need to, it starts on its own: 'the bed vibrated, the needles danced over the skin, the harrow moved gently up and down' [120/150]. Even the noisy cogwheel seems to have adapted to the new circumstances, since the functioning of the machine is quite silent.

Silent, but unruly, insubordinate after all. Its cogwheels begin to separate themselves from the system, as if they are being squeezed out of the machine. A large wheel rises into view, falls from the designer and rolls across the sand. Then another, 'followed by many others, big ones and little ones and ones that were hard to distinguish, with all of them the same thing happened; one kept thinking, surely at least by now the designer must be empty, but then a new, particularly numerous group appeared, rose up, fell to the ground, rolled along the sand and toppled over' [120–121/151].

Thoroughly absorbed by this spectacle of disintegration, the traveller hasn't been watching what the rest of the machine is doing. 'A new and still more disagreeable surprise' awaits him [121/151]. The harrow is not writing on the officer's body, neither 'Be just' nor any other sentence, it is just stabbing. The traveller, and indeed Kafka's narrative itself, now seem to want to make a particularly grisly and scholastic distinction. This is not torture ('*Folter*'), 'such as the officer had wished to achieve', but unmediated murder ('*unmittelbarer Mord*'). As if the machine was not dedicated, in its very conception, to both torture and murder, torture as murder. As if torture was martyrdom, and murder merely immoral.

The officer is dead, his body impaled on the harrow, on his face not the least sign of the transfiguration he so eagerly described as occurring in other cases. 'It was as it had been in life ... What all the others had found in the machine the officer had not found; his lips were pressed firmly together, his eyes were open and had the expression of life, their look was calm and convinced, through his forehead went the point of the great iron spike' [121/152].

In a brief epilogue the traveller visits the colony's teahouse, where the grave of the former Commandant is, curiously, to be found under one of the tables. The traveller leaves the teahouse, and hurries to the harbour, where he takes a small boat that will transport him to his steamer. The story ends as the former prisoner and his guard try to board the boat as well, and the traveller repels them with a heavy piece of rope, as if to cut off all human traces of the event he has witnessed.

III

The officer insists on the transparency of the glass harrow, which means that everyone can see how the inscription is completed on the body, and on the combination of long and short needles in the harrow itself: 'It is the long one that writes, and the short one squirts out water to wash away the blood and keep the script clear at all times' [106/134]. The script is readable, then, and meant to be read; but not read by anyone in the present time of the story. When it is read it is meant to produce the spectacle of an elaborate and ironic justice, a verbal matching of punishment to crime; but only a spectacle, and there are no spectators now except the isolated traveller.

And of course the spectators are not the central players here, or the chief readers, and we need to pause over the puzzle of torture as inscription. It is improbable but not impossible that the officer is right about the transfiguration of the sixth hour, since pain has been known to be a way of illumination, and the lives of many saints suggest as much. But the officer is also asking the traveller to believe that each punished body knows its particular, graphically appropriate sentence, that pain, or rather the aftermath of pain, or a supplement to pain ('For the first six hours the condemned man survives almost as before, he merely suffers pain' [108/136]) affords a precise, construable alphabet, a kind of Braille system of torment. What the spectators read through the glass harrow is grisly enough, particularly if we imagine the blood which is constantly washed away, but the act of reading even in this case is perfectly orthodox: one recognizes letters as they form, puts them together into words. But for the body to read an inscription through its wounds – to 'decipher' it, to use the officer's word – a special talent would be needed, a feeling literacy.

There is a danger of being too refined here. Kafka no doubt wants us to remember the brutality of these procedures in spite of (or because of) the normalizing language the characters use. We can and must say that the condemned man doesn't read anything, he is just cruelly tortured in the name of a fastidious, verbally infatuated legality. No one except the spectators and the operator reads anything, and only they are in a position to enjoy the irony, the 'poetic' justice. But it would be unlike Kafka to leave us with so broad a point, not to invite other angles of vision. The brutality and pain do not disappear in these other views, but the idea of the body reading remains, not as satire or inspired nonsense, but as a figure for a knowledge of the law which would be corporal and irrefutable. That this knowledge doesn't appear in the story except in the officer's affirmations, that it can't appear even there except as a fantasy, a kind of transfer of the spectators' literacy on to the suffering body of the victim, that even if it could appear within the 'reality' of the story it would be inseparable from pain and death – all this may be understood as an expression of longing for the law rather than a refusal or undoing of it.

The attraction of the officer's explanations for the traveller – and perhaps for us, too in some none too flattering way – is their conversion of confusion into directness, elaborate argument into immediate action. The present case is 'quite simple', the officer says, 'as they all are' [105/132]. But the officer's, and the system's, gift for simplification is seen at its most stretched and most powerful in the exhibition of the drawings ('*die Zeichnungen*') which represent the instructions for setting the sentences in the machine. They were made by the old Commandant.

The officer keeps the drawings, his 'most precious possession', in a leather case, and can't let the traveller touch them. He holds up a sheet. All the traveller can see is 'a maze of criss-cross lines'. 'Read it,' the officer says. The traveller says that he can't. 'But it's quite clear', the officer says. 'It's very artistic,' the traveller says, 'but I can't decipher it.' The officer seems quite pleased with this failed result, and laughs as he puts the drawings away.

It's no copy-book lettering for school children. It needs to be perused for a long time ... Of course it can't be any simple script; it's not supposed to kill straight away ... So the actual lettering has to be surrounded with many, many decorations; the text itself forms only a narrow band running round the body; the rest of the body is set aside for the embellishments. [107/135–136]

This account of the text makes the idea of the body reading it even more fantastic – the very thought that wounds would allow us to distinguish between a script and its embellishments is dizzying – but it also transfers the scene of reading away from both the spectators and the actual condemned man. What the officer reads easily, what the traveller can't decipher in the maze of lines, is a project of writing, a dream of the body become text. The drawings, ostensibly instructions for whoever sets the machine, are the map of an imaginary justice, where it is the script that kills, not the needles. What the law writes on the torn body of Damiens the regicide, described at the beginning of Michel Foucault's *Surveiller et punir*, is the power of the king and the force of an example, the public fact of crime. What the law writes on the body of condemned men in the penal colony, in the officer's idealizing view, is a verbal truth which transcends words, an unimaginable proximity to the law itself. If his body had been able to read his own sentence, the officer would not only have been instructed to be just, he would have been converted into a living (and then dead) emblem not of justice but of its exclusive and mortal pursuit.

IV

A word about the notion of impossibility in Kafka's fiction. There are many representations there of what we take to be material impossibilities: a talking horse, a talking ape, a singing mouse, a short bridge that runs straight from New York to Boston, a Statue of Liberty who holds not a torch

but a sword in her hand. I'm unsure whether this last instance
is a simple mistake, a Freudian slip or an inspired rewriting
of American iconography – perhaps it's all three. But there is
also a particular kind of impossibility of which I think Kafka
may be the inventor, although many other practitioners have
worked with it since. It's the impossibility that occurs when
you are arrested but still allowed to go about your business;
when a body is said to read what it could not conceivably
read, even metaphorically. It's the impossibility, to take an
example from one of Kafka's heirs, that occurs when you are
declared dead by the American army, in *Catch-22*, and none
of the ordinary signs of life – blood pressure, temperature,
occupation of physical space, ability to shout and argue with
your colleagues, and write letters to your wife – is allowed to
combat this declaration. You are dead because you are called
dead, even if everything else about you says that you are
alive.[19] Another, perhaps less likely, heir is Luis Buñuel, and
there is a scene in his film *The Phantom of Liberty* which
elaborates exactly the same kind of impossibility. Two
Parisian parents are alarmed to receive a telephone call
informing them that their little girl is missing from school.
They rush to the scene, and the headmistress tells them that
she doesn't understand what has happened. The girls were all
there when they were counted, but now Aliette has suddenly
and mysteriously disappeared. The headmistress leads them
to a classroom and takes the register. The girls all call out
'Present', including the supposedly missing Aliette. 'See,' the
headmistress says. 'She's there on the register.' No one pays
any attention to the live Aliette. The parents' consternation
is as strong as it was, the evidence of their eyes and ears

[19] Joseph Heller, *Catch-22*. New York: Simon & Schuster, 2003,
pp. 351–355.

irrelevant. They go to a police station to report the case, taking the girl with them. The commissioner gives instructions for a search, and two dizzying Buñuel jokes occur in very fast succession. Aliette is made to stand in front of the commissioner, so that he can get an exact description of the missing person. He even asks her questions. And the policeman who is to conduct the search asks if he can take Aliette with him – so he will recognize her when he sees her. The commissioner says, 'No, no, just look at her closely. And start the search immediately.'[20]

I should like to call this kind of impossibility a logical one, but that isn't quite right. Something has gone wrong with the relation of ordinary words to the world, and it's not at all clear whether the trouble lies in the words or in the world. Perhaps in both, and in their relation, too. Either 'arrested' (or 'reading' or 'dead' or 'missing' – these are not outlandish words) doesn't mean what it usually means, or its usual sense has dispensed with any need for reference, released itself, like Hitler or Kafka's father, from all connection to the demands and controls of empirical reality. Either we scramble for a new, special meaning of the word, or the word means just what it likes, whatever conditions obtain.

In the grisliest of these cases, the one represented by 'In the Penal Colony', we struggle to imagine a body reading through its pain. This is not impossible: we can imagine a metaphorical sense of reading which will stretch this far – after all, we are used to thinking of pain as a signal. But then we have to imagine the same body reading literally, not 'reading' but reading, actual sentences: 'Honour Thy Superiors'; 'Be Just'. Reading them, in most cases, in a foreign language, one the mind itself doesn't know, let

[20] Luis Buñuel, *Le fantôme de la liberté*. Greenwich Films, 1974.

alone the body. And worse or more impossible still, we have to imagine that the same body can distinguish such sentences from mere curlicues and squiggles of decoration.

We can't do this. We can interpret the impossibility, but we can't interpret it as possible. It's hard enough here to contemplate the pain and torture in general, the cruelty of the colony – to lay hold of it mentally, as Conrad says of another horror. But Kafka is asking even more of us. And even less. He wants us to imagine not only various readings of the impossible such as I sketched earlier, but something simpler and more drastic: the impossible itself. Not the apparently, contingently impossible but the radically, categorically, non-sensically impossible. The act of imagining this would have been, will be, good practice for history's next revision of the syllabus, when what we thought was impossible happens yet again.

CHAPTER 4

Seven types of obliquity

I

In this chapter I want to borrow a bit of method from William Empson, and so my title is not just a joking homage – although of course it is that – but an attempt, by sympathetic magic, to get Empson's backing for what I'm trying to do.

But just what is the method of *Seven Types of Ambiguity*? You will remember that in both Conrad's *Heart of Darkness* and Coppola's *Apocalypse Now*, Kurtz's method is described as 'unsound'. In the novella Marlow asks, 'Do you call it "unsound method"?' The other person says, 'Don't you?' and Marlow murmurs, 'No method at all.'[1] People in most scientific disciplines would say that Empson's method was no method at all, and so would many semiologists and people working in stylistics. Empson himself was rather offhand about the method but devoted to it all the same. Its main element was close reading, of course, an agile and intense, inspired and sometimes perverse attention to particular passages from poems and plays, and I can't do anything with that except salute it with enormous gratitude, and return to

---

[1] Joseph Conrad, *Heart of Darkness*. New York: Norton, 1971, p. 63. Francis Ford Coppola, *Apocalypse Now*. Zoetrope, 1979.

the book again and again, and invite you to do the same. We can all try our hand at close reading, but you have to be Empson to read like Empson. Here I want to defend the principle of the seven types itself, I think, of great methodological interest.

First, because the number seven represents both specificity and open-endedness. Apart from the echoes of old numerological symbolisms, as in the seven hills of Rome and the seven deadly sins, in a secular world the number seven suggests both an identifiable set of instances and a sense that the barrel is far from scraped. If there are seven types, there could be more, and probably are – not an infinite number, perhaps, but plenty.

Second, the types do distinguish different forms of ambiguity but the types are not the point. Ambiguity is the point, and the profusion of closely discussed examples. The types are a convenience, a logical device and not an ambitious or supposedly durable taxonomy.

Third, the types are not just a convenience, they tell a story, they represent an ascending order of complexity, from relatively straightforward instances of double or multiple meanings in words – well, as straightforward as instances of ambiguity can get – all the way to cases where the mind of the writer is torn apart, and the meanings of the words in turn tear at each other. A famous example is Empson's reading of the word 'buckle' in Hopkins's poem 'The Windhover'. The word, Empson said, meant both buckle as one buckles a belt, and buckle like a bicycle wheel. He afterwards said that he thought this was 'the only really disagreeable case in the book'; that he now felt Hopkins couldn't have meant anything of the kind; and that if the ambiguity had been pointed out to him, Hopkins would 'after much conscientious self-torture' have destroyed the poem.[2] But the whole point about ambiguities in language, and one of my reasons for so persistently personifying literature, is that words organized into sentences live in a shared historical world rather than in anyone's private control. It's clear that Hopkins meant buckle as one buckles a belt – in part because there is a pub called The Hawk and Buckle quite near the college where Hopkins was pursuing his theological studies. It's also clear, I think, that if we know the other meaning of the word it must shadow what is being said, whether Hopkins meant it to or not, and the shadow is entirely consistent with the poem's worries. If you are suggesting, as the poem does, that a disciplined hawk resting on the wrist is even more beautiful than a hawk flying free in the open sky, and by analogy that the rigorously subdued heart is more beautiful than a heart enjoying what looks like its natural liberty, the double meaning allows us another, secret view, and doesn't contradict, but complicates the main claim. The types, then, permit Empson not just to arrange his examples but to make something of the arrangement.

And fourth, in only apparent contradiction to what I have just said, Empson shows a cheerful, indeed alarming, willingness to play around with his own categories, to think he may have placed an example in the wrong type, or that the types may after all not be so different from each other. There are several comic moments of this kind in the book, and the procedure may seem just reckless. 'In a sense the sixth class is included within the fourth'; 'The last example of my fourth chapter belongs by rights either to the fifth or

[2] William Empson, *Seven Types of Ambiguity*. Norfolk: New Directions, 1966, p. 226.

to the sixth.'[3] I have to say I find the procedure admirable.
What it says, I think, is that the types are not nothing, but
that they are not everything either. It is possible to need
them (most of the time) and to let them go (occasionally).
This is itself how ambiguity works for Empson, in life as in
literature. In its broadest description it is a way of believing
two contradictory things at once; in daily practice it offers a
way of making choices and remembering what the alternatives were. He evokes, for instance, 'a generous scepticism which can believe at once that people are and are not
guilty', and calls this 'a very normal and essential method'.
'This sort of contradiction,' he said, 'is at once understood
in literature.'

People, often, cannot have done both of two things, but they must
have been in some way prepared to have done either; whichever
they did, they will have still lingering in their minds the way they
would have preserved their self-respect if they had acted differently; they are only to be understood by bearing both possibilities
in mind.[4]

Put together, the four points I have enumerated – there should
be seven, but I'm not going to get there – offer us a dynamic
and subtle model of literary response. We can multiply and
then count the possibilities of interpretation, and also think
there might be more. We can believe that our instances matter
more than our arrangements of them. We can believe that the
arrangements, too, are interesting. And if we are lucky, we can
manage to be flexible and nontrivial at the same time. This is
not a bad programme. The difficulty is getting anywhere near
it in practice.

[3] Empson, *Seven Types of Ambiguity*, p. 190.
[4] Ibid., p. 44.

II

The gist of the argument of this chapter, as you probably suspect, is that obliquity is unavoidable in literature but that some of it can seem pretty direct. What I want to try and show is how this happens. Several of my instances of obliquity are here because I think they have a strong interest and appeal in their own right, and they are considerably richer in themselves than anything I can say about them. This is entirely in keeping with one of the major themes of this book – that we have perceptions, as Henry James says, that we cannot translate into words, and especially moral and critical perceptions – but I also agree that this line can seem a little too easy, and I'm not artfully trying to fail to say things, I'm just doing what I can.

I've grouped the seven types in this way. Three types of what seem like very direct language in literature: affirmation, instruction and query. Two very general types of literary behaviour: figurative language and questioning of genre. And finally two types of obliquity in interpretation, one based on the sense that literary cases can't be closed, and one based on the way a good deal of literature seems, as we interpret it, to turn into parable. The last point is tendentious, and needs a lot more working out. I'm not sure whether literature keeps turning into parable, or whether modern readers keep wanting it to. Literature may have plans of its own.

An affirmation, as I suggested in an earlier chapter, seems about as far from obliquity as you can get and still be in a poem or a novel or a play. 'All happy families are alike ...' 'About suffering they were never wrong,/The Old Masters ...' 'It is a truth universally acknowledged ... that a person discussing assertions of this kind will sooner

or later quote Jane Austen.' These propositions and propositions like them, I have been suggesting, are soundings rather
than dogma, and just agreeing with them, nodding sagely, or
writing 'How true' in the margin of the text, is surely too
passive a response, and can be seen as a form of misreading –
or subreading. But I've been suggesting, too, that just bracket-
ing off such statements as 'literature', seeing them as making
claims not subject to any verification except the kind that
comes from within the work itself (internal consistency,
power of persuasion or conviction within a particular context), is also a form of misreading, or a way of missing much
that matters. Now comes the hard part. How do we read
them, if we are actually, actively reading? Well, with a
mixture of scepticism and belief; of trust in fiction and
awareness of fakery; of submission to syntax and imagery
and alertness to technique, of dependence on internal cross-
reference and constant checking with our often rather
casually held notions about lived historical life. There is
much more in the mixture. This mixture is very easy to
manage – we do it all the time – but it looks very weird, and
perhaps impossible, when you describe it.

Let me return briefly to Auden's poem 'Musée des
Beaux Arts', and its opening claim that the Old Masters
were never wrong about suffering. We may think that the
Old Masters were human, and probably wrong sometimes,
even about suffering, and then we shall, pretty casually,
take the phrase as a hyperbole. 'Never wrong' means
'usually right'. We may also, reading through the poem,
feel that it was not exactly suffering that the Old Masters
were usually right about. They were right, perhaps, about
the way dogs go on with their doggy lives and people, too,
go on with their doggy lives; about the way many people,
perhaps most people, react to the exceptional event. They

ignore it. The Old Masters knew, Brueghel knew, 'how everything turns away / Quite leisurely from the disaster'. Icarus has fallen from the sky, but nobody is paying attention. That's what the painting shows, and that's what the poem says, too.

Several interpretative moves are available to us here. First, we may feel the Old Masters were right, and assent rather grimly, or indeed with a sour satisfaction, to their view of human indifference. As long as we'd thought about this, it wouldn't be quite the same as nodding sagely and saying, 'How true.' Second, we might feel, as I do, and as I have tried to indicate, that we want the Old Masters to be wrong in their view of the human relation to the exceptional event, but can't believe them to be entirely mistaken – what we know of history gets in the way of our kindly wish. So we feel they are not wrong enough; not as wrong as we want and perhaps even need them to be. Third, we may believe the Old Masters are indeed quite wrong in their view, and then we summon up all the counter-instances, roll out our lists of acts of attention, unsung bravery and uncalled-for deeds of compassion. We could get quite indignant about this, and very cross with the Old Masters, and perhaps with Auden.

There are many more possible reactions apart from these three, of course, but I think this limited sample shows schematically how affirmation works in a poem. It is a genuine affirmation, not a pretend or pseudo one, and we can argue about it in the way we might argue, late at night in the kitchen, about whether Stanley Kubrick was a genius or the most boring filmmaker of all time. But unlike a human arguer, the poem doesn't need to be right, and what it knows is different from what it says. It knows there is a good chance that many people will think its affirmation is right, and that even those who disagree with it will think the argument matters. I'm not sure what we would call the knowledge of a good chance. I think technically we have to call it guessing, but it's hard not to feel it is some sort of knowledge after all.

III

Here's a second type of obliquity which also looks fairly direct. It is the mode of instruction, and I evoked some examples of this, too, earlier. 'Lose something every day', Elizabeth Bishop says in a poem that I discuss in my next chapter. 'Accept the fluster/ of lost door keys, the hour badly spent . . . / Then practice losing farther, losing faster . . .' 'You must change your life', Rilke says (*'Du mußt dein Leben ändern'*). Strictly, it is an ancient torso of Apollo that says this in the poem, it hasn't got a head and it couldn't talk if it had. But I don't think any reader of the poem has failed to experience this sentence as a direct and startling personal address. The question is not whether the instruction is meant for us but whether we have been able to do anything about it. I have never managed to change my life in the way I thought the poem was telling me to, but I never thought the poem wasn't telling me to get on with it.

But surely then this is not literature at all but wisdom, counsel or moral instruction. I don't think any of these things is beyond the reach of literature, but Rilke's imperative is literary because it is so peculiarly intimate. It knows us well without knowing us at all. It speaks not of life and change in general but of the specific lived life and probably failed change of each of us. It is both direct and indirect, just like the personal pronoun it uses. Nothing more intimate than the word 'you', addressed to a single individual. 'Only you', as the terrible old popular song goes. Nothing more endlessly indirect, less tied to a particular reference, than a pronoun. Rilke is a name, but 'we' are whoever we are.

But let's look at a more complicated example. This is Sonnet 13 of the Second Part of the *Sonnets to Orpheus*, 1922, and one of the very greatest of Rilke's poems. What follows is a fairly literal prose translation of my own. One contextual point, interesting in the light of this discussion, is that this poem is flanked by two poems that also begin with an imperative. Sonnet 12 says 'Will the change' ('*Wolle die Wandlung*') and Sonnet 14 says 'Look at the flowers ('*Siehe die Blumen*').

Be ahead of all farewells, as though they were behind you like the winter that is just passing. For among winters there is one that is so endlessly winter that, if you survive it, your heart will survive altogether.

Be always dead in Eurydice, rise back with more singing, with more praise, into pure relation. Here, among what vanishes, in the realm of decline, be a sounding glass that broke into pieces as it sounded.

Be – and at the same time know what the condition of not-being is, the unending ground of your inmost movement, so that you may fully complete it this single time.

To the worn and dull and mute supply of ample nature, to the unsayable sums, add yourself in celebration, and destroy the reckoning.[5]

---

[5] Here is the German text:

> Sei allem Abscheid voran, als wäre er hinter
> dir, wie der Winter, der eben geht.
> Denn unter Wintern ist einer so endlos Winter,
> daß, überwinternd, dein Herz überhaupt übersteht.
>
> Sei immer tot in Eurydike – , singender steige,
> preisender steige zurück in den reinen Bezug.

It would take days to develop even the beginning of a close reading of this poem, but let me try to say something briefly about its instructions. About their addressee, first of all. This must be Orpheus, because the title of the volume tells us so, and he is the one who is going to be always dead in Eurydice – or who is being told to be. It is almost certainly Rilke himself as well, and perhaps a more generic figure of the modern poet; and of course it is us, since once we have read the poem we can't pretend we weren't there. But then how do we read the instructions, and how does instruction compare with affirmation?

'Be ahead of all farewells', 'Be always dead in Eurydice', 'be a sounding glass', 'Be' and 'add yourself to the unsayable sums'. The sense of intimacy persists, as in the phrase about changing our lives. The poem knows us well without knowing us at all, or I would say in this case, it knows our needs, it knows we have been denying death in all kinds of hopeless ways. I remember the philosopher Gillian Rose reading this poem aloud during a lecture not long before she died. She knew she was dying, and she clearly took the poem as meaning that she should make her death part of her life, not see it as an invasion of the unthinkable or an absurdity. 'This appeal', she said of the poem's urging, 'holds out no

> *Hier, unter Schwindenden, sei, im Reich der Neige,*
> *sei ein klingendes Glas, das sich im Klang schon zerschlug.*
>
> *Sei- und wisse sogleich des Nicht-Seins Bedingung,*
> *den unendlichen Grund deiner innigen Schwingung,*
> *daß du sie völlig vollziehst dieses einziges Mal.*
>
> *Zu dem gebrauchten sowohl, wie zum dumpfen und stummen*
> *Vorrat der vollen Natur, den unsäglichen Summen,*
> *zähle dich jubelnd hinzu und vernichte die Zahl.*

Rainer Maria Rilke, *Ausgewählte Gedichte*. Frankfurt: Suhrkamp, 1966, p. 162.

impersonal, endless dying.' And (of the condition of not-being): 'This knowledge does not fall into the opposition of mastery/passivity.'[6] Empson once said that Tennyson's 'Tithonus' was 'a poem in favour of the human practice of dying'.[7] Rilke's poem knows that we can't be in favour of dying, and also that it makes a difference whether the death is our own or someone else's. But it knows, too, as Rilke wrote in an extraordinary phrase, that 'death is the side of life that is turned away from us'.[8] All of the poem's instructions invite us to imagine perishing and the perishable as forms of life, and they are in this sense not at all like the affirmation in Auden's poem. They are oblique not because they leave room for argument, or guess there is a chance of our thinking they are right, but because they ask so much work of us, and scarcely tell us where to start.

IV

And now a form of obliquity which is grammatically direct but doesn't seem to take its directness too seriously, and not just because I am taking my examples from Yeats. I have in mind the rhetorical question, of which Yeats was such a master. Just think of all those wonderful, famous lines:

> Who will go drive with Fergus now?
>
> Was there another Troy for her to burn?

---

[6] Gillian Rose, *Mourning Becomes the Law*. Cambridge: Cambridge University Press, 1996, pp. 145, 146.

[7] Quoted by John Haffenden in the notes to William Empson, *The Complete Poems*. London: Penguin, 2001, p. 347.

[8] From a letter to Witold Hulewicz, cited in the notes to *Selected Poetry*. Translated by Stephen Mitchell. New York: Vintage, 1989, p. 319.

What shall I do with this absurdity –
O heart, O troubled heart – this caricature,
Decrepit age that has been tied to me
As to a dog's tail?

What if those things the greatest of mankind
Consider most to magnify, or to bless,
But take our greatness with our bitterness?

Did she put on his knowledge with his power?

How can we know the dancer from the dance?

Did that play of mine send out
Certain men the English shot?

And stealthiest of all because it doesn't look like a question until we reach the end of the sentence (and the poem), indeed isn't a question until it is converted into one by a piece of punctuation, is the following even more famous instance. The syntax seems to say, 'I know ... what rough beast ... slouches towards Bethlehem to be born.' But it turns out that we are to read, 'What rough beast ... slouches towards Bethlehem to be born?' Here's how the double syntax goes:

> I know
> That twenty centuries of stony sleep
> Were vexed to nightmare by a rocking cradle,
> And [I also know] what rough beast [etc.].

Or:

> I know
> That twenty centuries of stony sleep
> Were vexed to nightmare by a rocking cradle,
> And [I need to ask] what rough beast [etc.].[9]

[9] W. B. Yeats, *Collected Poems*. Edited by Richard J. Finneran. Basingstoke: Macmillan, 1989, pp. 43, 91, 195, 201, 215, 217, 345, 187.

These questions are different again from affirmations and instructions. Because they are questions, first of all, but also because they propose a different relation between words and things, and between text and reader. Paul de Man argued that all literature is rhetorical in the way in which these questions are rhetorical, that is, suspended between asking and not asking, hovering between different points of reference, and therefore undecidable in their meaning.[10] Strictly, I think that literary meanings are undecided until a reader decides them, and that in many interesting cases they could be decided differently. But that doesn't make them undecidable: it makes decisions indispensable. De Man may have been guilty of what Empson was always being accused of doing: confusing possible meanings with plausible or actual meanings. Empson merely thought that we shouldn't rush to the plausible until we had had a good look at the possible. And that such a look might, and probably should, change our idea of what the plausible is.

A good way of seeing how these questions work will be to take what seems the simplest and least rhetorical of them – especially since we have some distinguished answers to the question to hand.

> Did that play of mine send out
> Certain men the English shot?

Yeats is referring to his play *Cathleen ni Houlihan*, 1902, and Stephen Gwynn wrote in 1936 that the effect of the play on

---

[10] 'The grammatical model of the question becomes rhetorical ... when it is impossible to decide ... which of the two meanings (that can be entirely incompatible) prevails. Rhetoric radically suspends logic and opens up vertiginous possibilities of referential aberration.' Paul de Man, *Allegories of Reading*. New Haven: Yale University Press, 1979, p. 10.

him was to send him home asking himself 'if such plays should be produced unless one was prepared for people to go out and shoot and be shot'.[11] A figure representing Auden in a poem by Paul Muldoon has a more emphatic, rhyming response to the same question. The answer is: 'Certainly not.' 'If Yeats had saved his pencil-lead/would certain men have stayed in bed?'[12] Auden, you will remember, is the poet whose in Memory of W. B. Yeats', insists that 'poetry makes nothing happen'.[13] In an elegant if dizzying twist on the question, commenting on the Muldoon poem, Denis Donoghue says that the answer is 'certainly not "certainly not"'.[14] But where does this leave us?

The question acts, I think, in a manner that is the precise opposite of the instruction in Rilke. The instruction is general, applies to us all, but seeks us out through its grammar, and its apparently intimate knowledge of our needs. Yeats's question is personal, about himself and his writing, about a particular play and a particular rebellion, and identifiable dead men; but it becomes active only when we generalize it, when we worry, as Yeats constantly did, about the relation of the world of literature to the world of action, and specifically about the relation of plays and poems to violence. As with Rilke's instructions, we need to do quite a bit of work here, but the work is different, less inward, directed more to our sense of history than to our capacity to imagine change and death. This isn't true of all the questions I quoted, but it is

---

[11] Quoted by Richard Finneran in his notes to *Collected Poems*, p. 514.

[12] Paul Muldoon, *Poems*, 1968–1998, p. 178.

[13] W. H. Auden, *Collected Poems*, Faber & Faber, 1991, p. 248.

[14] 'It is entirely possible that some members of the audience at *Cathleen ni Houlihan* felt impelled to take up arms in a nationalist cause already well established.' Denis Donoghue, 'Yeats: the New Political Issue', *Princeton University Library Chronicle*, vol. 59, no. 3, Spring 1998, p. 364.

true of most of them, and of some of the least likely ones, including the ones about Troy and the rough beast. The second Troy we can't imagine itself marks a historical gap, a missing stage of action for a remarkable individual woman. The beast, when it arrives, will have chosen a quite specific historical Bethlehem of its own. What's oblique here is a proposed relation to knowledge in its most ordinary sense; knowledge of what happens in the world and what may or may not happen again; what we know and we think we know. The literary question, in this framework, is not opposed to affirmation, but it is different, in exactly the way that speculation is different from argument.

V

I'm going to talk about figurative language in the form of a small confession, or an apology for my own recourse to a particular figure of speech. A number of friends and colleagues with whom I have discussed the subject of this book have objected strenuously to my use of personification. I say that I am trying to ask what literature knows, if it knows anything, and if knowledge is the right word for what is in question, and they say that literature doesn't know or not know anything, only people do that, writers and readers. Personifying literature is just mischievous, fanciful, an obfuscation or a mystification, a hiding of the real issues. I don't mind the figure being mischievous or fanciful, but I don't want it to obfuscate or mystify or hide anything. My hope is that it will serve as a kind of shorthand – shorthand for more things, and more various things, than I can otherwise keep mentioning at the same time.

Still, it will be good to try to mention some of them, at least once, if only to show that the shorthand is not sleight of hand, or not meant to be. We can unpack, as they say, the figure of speech. And we can look at the figure of speech at work – since each personification, I believe, entails a rather different person.

By treating literature as a person I am suggesting that literature has a life of its own. I don't mean anything grand or romantic by this, and I'm not suggesting spontaneous self-creation. The writer is the sufficient and necessary cause of any piece of writing. But all utterances, all pieces of language have a potential life of their own, in the sense that they can, in addition to what their speakers or writers mean and what their listeners or readers take them to mean, mean something else entirely. Jacques Derrida says that this is the basic fact about writing. '*Tout graphème est d'essence testamentaire*' ('every piece of writing is essentially a will or a testament').[15] The writer has gone away, and left it behind, at the mercy of the world. This is true of Shakespeare's sonnets, but also true of the note on the door which says, 'Back in a minute', which could be torn down, or with a little ingenuity taken to be a fragment of a larger message, for instance, 'She sent the engagement ring back in a minute cardboard box.' I would want to say that this alienation or straying of meaning is a basic possibility of all language – a possibility mostly obscured by the practical uses we put language to, and by the sheer efficiency and success of language as an instrument. But efficiency and success are not everything. We can misspeak, as in Freudian slips; we can misspeak on purpose, creating puns. And we can go in for multiple misspeaking

[15] Jacques Derrida, *De la grammatologie*. Paris: Editions de Minuit, 1967, p. 100.

and mishearing, creating and finding Empsonian ambiguity, alias literature in one of its important aspects. This is not a view of literature which kills off or disempowers either writer or reader; it just reminds them of their medium.

Their medium. There is an important continuity from ordinary language to literature. Or more precisely, ordinary language is full of small examples of literature, or of the literary, as the Russian formalists would say. Irony, fiction, metaphor, rhyme, alliteration: you can't get very far into the day without running into some or all of these. 'Up early today', your wife says when you roll out of bed at eleven. 'Are you in training for the marathon?' You say, 'I had a rough night. Tossing and turning. I thought payday was never going to come.' Irony, fiction, metaphor, alliteration, rhyme – in that order.

But there is another sense in which we need to refuse or complicate this continuity, and that is something else my personification of literature is meant to suggest. The literary is everywhere, but literature is a formalized concentration of the literary, and the degree of formalization is significant. Sometimes the formal element is very obvious – in a sonnet or a villanelle, for instance, and indeed in pretty much all verse, even terrible verse. Sometimes it's less obvious, a matter of tone or inflection, or noncoercive plot, and of course the whole triumph of the realist novel rests on its ability to bury or deny its formal properties, to behave as if it were just letting us look in on an unaltered, unshaped world. The very things that now seem to us so natty, so beautifully designed in *Middlemarch* or *Anna Karenina* – say, the lovely montage effects of the switches between the different storylines, as cinematic as anything in Flaubert or Griffith – were once taken as the raw, unmanaged stuff of life itself. But the element of form is always there in literature, and it is what makes the work a work. It is, we might say, the difference between a draft and a finished project, and here of course the craft and skill and labour of the writer are essential. But then a work of any kind – poem or sonata or table or hat – must have a certain independence from its maker, and writers are endlessly, ruefully talking about this. Readers, on the other hand, are likely to feel this independence makes literature what it is.

A last use for my personification of literature. It reminds us that reading is, or can be, an act of creation. What happens when we read literature is that what the author knows and what we know form, in combination, something new, a third quantity, which we may or may not want to call knowledge. This new quantity is born in the moment of reading itself, as Martha Nussbaum, in *Love's Knowledge*, says love may be crystallised in a moment of perception. 'Love is not a structure in the heart waiting to be discovered.'[16] There are things waiting to be discovered in a novel or poem or play, and with luck we shall discover them. Similarly, we bring our whole affective and intellectual lives to the act of reading any text we care about. But the meeting produces something else again, or does in literature's best moments. What literature knows, what a novel or poem or play knows, is strictly, unfiguratively, what I now know that I didn't know before I read the text. Or what I only half-knew before; and perhaps even cannot now articulate as knowledge. And while this may well be less than what the author knew – and often is, alas – it may also be more, or different.

[16] Martha Nussbaum, *Love's Knowledge*. Oxford: Oxford University Press, 1992, pp. 267–268.

Personification also leads us to implied persons. Stathis Gourgouris asks a pertinent question in the title of his book *Does Literature Think?* but also seeks to go further:

The question is not simply whether literature thinks but whether literature thinks theoretically – whether it has a capacity to theorize the conditions of the world from which it emerges and to which it addresses itself. Moreover, underlying these premises is the question of literature's capacity to theorize ... without the aid of the analytical methods we have come to consider essential to theory.[17]

Gourgouris's whole book, which ranges from classical Greece to the novels of Don DeLillo, is an elegant if dense demonstration that literature can not only think theoretically, it can think like someone who has been reading Adorno, Benjamin and Derrida, along with Judith Butler and Edward Said.

Pierre Macherey's *A quoi pense la litterature?* takes for granted that literature does think, and his question really is more formal than it looks. He is asking about the relation between literary language and philosophical language, the *'rapport entre un discours littéraire et un discours philosophique'*. 'What form of thought is included in literary texts, and can it be extracted from them?' 'In a way I am proposing to defend the speculative vocation of literature.' That is, literature's vocation as an art of speculation. Perhaps the most interesting suggestion in the book is the proposition that 'literary philosophy ... is a form of thought without concepts'.[18]

---

[17] Stathis Gourgouris, *Does Literature Think?* Stanford: Stanford University Press, 2003, p. 2

[18] Pierre Macherey, *A quoi pense la littérature?* Paris: Presses universitaires de France, 1990, pp. 61, 8, 10, 198. My translation.

Of course, thinking is not knowing, but the titles of these books suggested looser boundaries to me than the books themselves drew. I liked the idea of asking literature not so much what it formally thought, but what sorts of things it was thinking of, what was on its mind. A penny for its thoughts.[19] The road leads me back to my adaptation of de Bolla's question: 'What does this painting know?'

This untouchable person-painting, hanging on to its secret, is different from Gourgouris's contemporary theorist and Macherey's conceptless philosopher. And from many other personifications, of course. Different, too, from my own rather diffuse figurative creature, who through the succeeding chapters of this book seems to know what a Henry James novel knows; what Hesiod's Muses know; what Kafka's prescient fiction knows; what the form of the villanelle knows; and whatever hides in the affirmations, instructions, inquiries, jokes and parables of a whole range of writers, as well as in the science of gaiety apparently espoused by Nietzsche and Yeats.

What sort of person would know these things? Someone a little less secretive than de Bolla's painting, perhaps. But it would have to be someone oblique, someone whose relation to life was real, even intense, but provisional, always subject to inversion or relocation. I am not, of course, suggesting that figurative language is all there is to literature, or that criticism has nothing but metaphors to offer us. But I do think that criticism has to keep trying to find the language it

[19] cf phrases like the following, which were obviously on my mind, or lying about in it: 'holding a variety of things in your mind', 'various incidental impressions wandering about in your mind', 'an elaborate and definite technique at the back of the author's mind', 'incompatible ways of feeling … that were lying about in his mind'. Empson, *Seven Types of Ambiguity*, pp. 238, 240, 171, 145.

needs, and that reading figurative language, with all its dangers and temptations to self-indulgence, is good practice for reading almost everything else.

VI

There is a dizzying moment in *The Real Life of Sebastian Knight*, by Vladimir Nabokov, when the narrator, who at no point gives us his name, but tells us only that its initial letter is V, writes something like this. 'I rang the bell, and when the door opened, a man appeared. I said my name was so-and-so, and he said his name was Pahl Pahlovitch Rechnoy.' We reconstruct the scene easily, and imagine the name we don't know as casually present in the narrated time of the story. V said who he was then but he's not saying now. Or he gave a false name but he's not telling us what it is. But in fact the narrator doesn't write this, only something like it, and in the end not all that much like it.

What he writes is not 'I said my name was so-and so', but, '"My name is so-and-so," I said.' 'And mine', his interlocutor cries, 'is Pahl Pahlovitch Rechnoy.'[20] It's not that the narrator's mask has slipped and revealed his true face, it's that his present mask has fallen into his past life, and with this move the whole narrative convention about the literal correctness of what appears between inverted commas is in ruins. V could have refused to give his name to Pahl Pahlovitch, as he refuses to give it to us, but he can scarcely, in any intelligible universe, have introduced himself as so-and-so.

Another example, which I think complements this one, and may help to make this strange type of obliquity clearer.

<hr>

[20] Vladimir Nabokov, *The Real Life of Sebastian Knight*. New York: New Directions, 1959, p. 142.

In Jean Rhys's novel *Good Morning, Midnight*, Sasha Jansen, the narrator and heroine, has just been sacked from her job as saleswoman in a Paris fashion shop. 'It was one of those dress-houses still with a certain prestige ... but its customers were getting fewer and fewer.' She gives the manager, the aptly or aggressively named Mr Blank, a piece of her mind before she goes, delivers an eloquent, extended tirade. Then she says, 'Did I say all this?' As soon as she asks, we know she didn't. She just thought it. Except that that is not quite what happens.

This is how Sasha Jansen describes her conversation:

Well, let's argue this out, Mr Blank. You, who represent Society, have the right to pay me four hundred francs a month. That's my market value, for I am an inefficient member of Society, slow in the uptake, uncertain, slightly damaged in the fray, there's no denying it. So you have the right to pay me four hundred francs a month, to lodge me in a small, dark room, to clothe me shabbily, to harass me with worry and monotony and unsatisfied longings till you get me to the point when I blush at a look, cry at a word. We can't all be happy, we can't all be rich, we can't all be lucky – and it would be so much less fun if we were. Isn't it so, Mr Blank? There must be the dark background to show up the bright colours. Some must cry so that others may be able to laugh the more heartily. Sacrifices are necessary ... Let's say that you have this mystical right to cut my legs off. But the right to ridicule me afterwards because I am a cripple – no, that I think you haven't got. And that's the right you hold most dearly, isn't it? You must be able to despise the people you exploit. But I wish you a lot of trouble, Mr Blank, and just to start off with, your damned shop's going bust. Alleluia! Did I say all this? Of course I didn't. I didn't even think it.[21]

[21] Jean Rhys, *Good Morning, Midnight*. London: Penguin, 1969, pp. 16, 25–26.

As with the Nabokov example, two times have been collapsed into one; the narrating present takes over the narrated past. There is only one time when we thought there were two. There is no confusion here on the narrator's part, as there is in Nabokov, no slippage or simulated slippage. This is a bold revision of the narrated life, a large insertion of new text into the story, a massive piece of *esprit d'escalier*. There is a broken rule in both cases, though, and it is the rule and its breaking that produces the startling effect. Fictional narrators can work in any tense they like, and they can interpolate comments to their hearts' content. But they are not supposed to let their present worries sneak into their reported dialogues, or to invent on the spot a whole chunk of what should have happened in the past. This looks like a breach of contract. It is, but it is also something else, something simpler.

We could say a lot more about the broken rule, but for the moment I want to look at another feature of these moments: the odd sense of privilege they give us, as if we were quite alone with the narrator, as if he and she have dropped their work for us, forgotten their story-telling manners, he because he is more worried about keeping his name from us than about telling his tale well, and she because she thinks, correctly, that we shall enjoy the bravura of her performance, whatever its relation to the reported event. But then what is the privilege here? We are not meeting the author, only a fully fictional narrator, and doesn't this encounter, in fact, happen all the time in lyric poetry? Isn't that just what a persona in lyric poetry is, someone who talks to us as if there were no one else there, and as if the time is always the present? Isn't that just how those instructions work in Rilke? Yes, but then why were we laughing or surprised? Not because these narrators are doing what they are doing, but because they are doing it here, suddenly, in a novel. The whole edifice of genre looks shaky.

And turns out to be quite solid, because it is shaken so rarely, because writers and readers are great observers of rules and codes.

VII

I want to close with two further types of obliquity which illustrate less the range or omnipresence of the condition than what many may feel is its literary heart: the obliquities that rest in the fact that readers of literature, interested as they are in propositions about the world, are often more interested in who is making them and why; and in the fact that much literature, *pace* Walter Pater, seems to aspire not to the condition of music but to the condition of parable.

Martha Nussbaum's book *Love's Knowledge* contains an elegant and persuasive account of what Proust is saying about knowledge. She says that he thinks it is what she, after Zeno, calls cataleptic. It comes to us through pain and suffering and is certain for that reason, knowledge in the heart; unlike the apparent, delusive knowledge offered to us by the reasoning mind. By Proust, Nussbaum means, she says, 'the author-in-the-text' rather than the 'real-life author', and she makes finely shaded statements such as 'The novel repeatedly claims that there are no truths that can be detached from the perspective of a human life and its concrete experiences.'[22] Nussbaum is drawn to this contextual view, although not finally to Proust's view of knowledge as cataleptic. I'm drawn to this view, too, and I share the suspicion of Proust's theory. Why then do I hesitate when I read phrases like the just-quoted 'The

---

[22] Nussbaum, *Love's Knowledge*, p. 253.

novel repeatedly claims', or shorter, more frequent phrases about a writer's 'ideas' or what the writer or the text 'states' or 'holds'. It's not that I object to the careful extraction of claims, ideas, statements and tenets from novels. On the contrary, I have been arguing that we need to do this, and in fact can scarcely help doing it, are doing it all the time, whether we think about it or not.

But there is something missing if we don't do more than that, and what is missing is not just the dramatized, instantiated life of the novel. What's missing from such language are the further questions that the philosophical propositions themselves generate. I think Proust himself, not just his narrator, and not even just the author-in-the-text, held the view of knowledge that Nussbaum identifies, but Proust's novel asks us to test the view not only against its chances of being true but against the whole structure of a personality which would need to hold such a view, and against a time and a place in which the view might seem banal or original, striking or even desperate. The novel's persons, places, events and long theoretical passages certainly add up to a philosophy of knowledge. But they also add up to what's wrong with that theory, if we think there is something wrong with it, and we are invited to put what's wrong back into the novel and see what it does to our interpretation of it. The persons and the plot, let's say, give us a proposition; the proposition, contextualized by our imagination of what a need for it would mean and what the local reach of it might be, gives us persons, and perhaps rather different persons from the ones we saw before. Proust's Marcel, for example, distinguishes carefully between different kinds of theories, the hypotheses of the intelligence and the hypotheses of fear. On the subject of his friend Albertine, who has just left him, the hypotheses of the intelligence are invariably complex, consoling and wrong, and the hypotheses of fear not only confirmed but confirmed beyond his worst imaginings. After telling us this Marcel writes:

But ... the fact that the intelligence is not the most subtle, powerful and appropriate instrument for grasping the truth is only one more reason in favour of starting with the intelligence rather than with the intuitions of the unconscious or with unquestioning faith in our premonitions. It is life which little by little, case by case, allows us to realize that what is most important for our hearts or our minds is taught us not by reason but by other powers. And then it is the intelligence itself, which, recognizing their superiority, uses its reasoning in order to abdicate in their favour, and accepts the role of collaborator and servant. Experimental faith.[23]

There is so much to say about this passage. I find its evocation of 'other powers', and the abdication of the intelligence, as creepy as Nussbaum does, creepier, perhaps. But then I want to ask about the mind which is travestying the very idea of intelligence in this way, where this mind has been, what its psychic history is, and how it defines its wants. I see that it is torn between an intense, pragmatic attention to individual cases and a longing just to let go of thinking altogether. I see that it has a certain hostility towards Bergsonian intuitionism, but also has a hankering for an orderly change of regime, as if those scary other powers were interested in due process. 'Experimental faith' is an extraordinary two-way signpost, pointing to a form of belief which would have the empirical

---

[23] Marcel Proust, *A la recherche du temps perdu*, 4 vols. Paris: Gallimard, 1989, vol. IV, p. 7. Translated by Peter Collier. *The Fugitive*. London: Penguin, 2002, p. 391. Translation slightly modified.

caution of science, and a science which would be willing to take the risks of belief.

The situation resembles the one we found in the Auden poem. The novel, like the poem, has an argument but doesn't have to win it. But the situation is also rather different, because of the novel's huge philosophical ambitions and because of the extraordinary density of its realized historical and psychological context. We are closer, perhaps, to the condition I evoked when trying to describe our relation to *The Wings of the Dove*, where the sheer, shifting richness of the novel's portrayal of the moral world defeated even the most subtle and sympathetic of moralizers. There was too much morality in the novel, so to speak, rather than too little. Or too many moralities, rather than too few. But I don't think we are tempted to speak of defeat when we speak of Proust; rather of something like a continuous, and endless, readjustment of focus, as we move from claim to pathology, and from pathology back to claim, and from claim to pathology again. In Henry James the case seems closed, but we have to keep reopening it. In Proust the case doesn't even begin to seem closed. But this may mean only that there are many ways of opening cases and failing to close them.

VIII

Italo Calvino's *Invisible Cities* is a work of fiction, and a narrative, and a masterpiece, but beyond that it's not entirely clear what it is. Its framing device is a series of conversations – eighteen conversations – between the Great Khan, the Emperor of the Tartars, and the Venetian Marco Polo, and the bulk of the work records Polo's descriptions of an extraordinary series of (probably) imaginary cities.

The Khan has an atlas which at first seems to be a straightforward historical counterpart to Polo's fabulous geographies. 'The Great Khan has an atlas where all the cities of the empire and the neighboring realms are drawn . . . ' But then we learn that the atlas 'reveals the form of cities that do not yet have a form or a name'. There are cities shaped like Amsterdam, York, New York, Los Angeles, Kyoto. The atlas 'contains also the maps of the promised lands visited in thought but not yet discovered or founded: New Atlantis, Utopia, the City of the Sea, Oceana, Tamoe, New Harmony, New Lanark, Icaria'. And it also contains 'the cities that menace in nightmares and maledictions: Enoch, Babylon, Yahooland, Butua, Brave New World'.[24] So the atlas is after all historical in a sense in which Polo's cities are not. Its cities have been thought of or made by someone else, do not exist only in Polo's (or Calvino's) narration.

The Khan gets gloomy at the end of the book, and wants to think only of nightmares and maledictions. 'It is all useless,' he says, 'if the last landing place can only be the infernal city, and it is there that, in ever-narrowing circles, the current is drawing us.' Polo answers, and these are the last words of the book:

The inferno of the living is not something that will be; if there is one, it is what is already here, the inferno where we live every day, that we form by being together. There are two ways to escape suffering it. The first is easy for many: accept the inferno and become such a part of it that you can no longer see it. The second is risky and demands constant vigilance and apprehension: seek and learn to recognize who and what, in the midst of the inferno, are not inferno, then make them endure, give them space.[25]

---

[24] Italo Calvino, *Le città invisibili*. Milan: Mondadori, 1993, pp. 137, 140, 163. *Invisible Cities*. Translated by William Weaver. New York: Harcourt Brace Jovanovich, 1974, pp. 135, 138, 164.

[25] *Le città invisibili*, pp. 163–164; *Invisible Cities*, p. 165.

This passage is moving and helpful because it is so clear, because we know how to read it, and because we see at once what it is saying to us. And yet we do this not in spite of its obliquity but because of it. What makes the obliquity seem to vanish is our skill in reading it. Here, in this work of fiction, are two historical people having imaginary conversations about imagined cities. They close with a reference to a place, hell, which is real or imaginary depending on your religious beliefs, and may in all kinds of ways be both real and imaginary, or at least real and metaphorical. When Marlowe's Faustus thinks he can trap Mephistopheles by asking him how he comes to be in Wittenberg when he is supposed to be in hell – Mephistopheles has just defined hell as the place where the damned are kept – Mephistopheles is almost desperate at Faustus's pathetic either-or logic. He says, 'Why this is hell, nor am I out of it.'[26] 'Myself am hell', Milton's Satan says, meaning that his pain is his hell, and will be with him wherever he goes.[27] Calvino's Polo manages to turn these tropes into ironic advice. Since we are in hell, and are hell, why not call it something else, and live happily ever after. This is not an option in any theological hell known to me, but then neither is the chance of finding elements in hell that are not hell. But that is the force of the shifting term, with its long secular afterlife. There are infernos now that don't feel like inferno to everyone.

I said before that it's not entirely clear what sort of work *Invisible Cities* is. I think that now we should say provisionally that it is a closely structured set of parables, but that we scarcely notice that these are parables as we are reading

[26] Christopher Marlowe, *Doctor Faustus*. London: Methuen, 1965, p. 84.
[27] John Milton, *Paradise Lost*, in *Poetical Works*. Oxford: Oxford University Press, 1969, p. 276.

them. There are many meanings of inferno, there are many infernos, and we pick our own instantly, thinking analogic-ally as if we were trained medieval scholastics. We work through what Polo identifies as the available responses to these infernos and the act of interpretation is so fast that it doesn't seem like interpretation at all. But it is. Ask any other reader of this passage which inferno they had in mind.

Elizabeth Costello, in J. M. Coetzee's recent book of that name, is a realist novelist who ends up in a parable. Here is what she says in a lecture about literary modernity, the writer's death of God:

> The word-mirror is broken, irreparably, it seems … There used to be a time, we believe, when we could say who we were. Now we are just performers speaking our parts. The bottom has dropped out. We could think of this as a tragic turn of events, were it not that it is hard to have respect for whatever was the bottom that dropped out – it looks to us like an illusion now, one of those illusions sustained only by the concentrated gaze of everyone in the room. Remove your gaze for but an instant, and the mirror falls to the floor and shatters.[28]

The turn of events is not tragic, but it is not happy. Costello is an Australian woman in her late sixties, the author of several novels, the best known of which is *The House on Eccles Street*, devoted to Molly Bloom. In Coetzee's book she lectures on the massive slaughter and torture of animals going on around the world, and on the all but total indiffer-ence of humans to what is happening. She receives an American prize, and gives a fierce talk. She lectures on a cruise ship and meets a former lover, an African novelist who is not writing any more, just lecturing. She goes to a

---

[28] J. M. Coetzee, *Elizabeth Costello: Eight Lessons*. London: Secker & Warburg, 2003, pp. 19–20.

conference in Amsterdam and wonders whether writers can become evil by imagining evil for their readers. She meditates on the corporal relations between goddesses and humans. And she arrives at an allegorical gate borrowed from Kafka's 'Before the Law'. In what is perhaps the most disturbing episode, she travels to Africa to visit her sister, a nun who is receiving an honorary degree. The sister delivers a blistering attack on the humanities, and particularly on novels, and in this context the ordinarily prickly and difficult Elizabeth Costello begins to seem like one of us. 'I do not need to consult novels,' the sister says in conversation after her talk, 'to know what pettiness, what baseness, what cruelty human beings are capable of. That is where we start, all of us ... If the study of mankind amounts to no more than picturing to us our darker potential, I have better things to spend my time on.'[29]

Costello recognizes the place of parable as soon as she gets there. She sees that it is full of 'Kafka business'. 'The wall, the gate, the sentry, are straight out of Kafka ... Kafka, but only the superficies of Kafka; Kafka reduced and flattened to parody.' Why Kafka? In spite of her earlier borrowing of Kafka's talking ape for her arguments about the treatment of animals (and as an allegory for the writer standing up and talking instead of writing), she is, as she thinks, 'no devotee of Kafka. Most of the time she cannot read him without impatience.' She wonders whether she has been placed in Kafka's world just because she doesn't like Kafka: 'the show is put together in this way *because* it is not her kind of show'.[30] This may be true, but she can address her complaint only to her author, since he and no one else put her there.

[29] Ibid., p. 128.   [30] Ibid., p. 209.

More substantially she is in Kafka's world because her life has been tending towards parable and has finally arrived there. But since this is Coetzee and not Calvino, there is none of the ease of interpretation we found with *Invisible Cities*: no ease of any kind. And since this is Coetzee and not Kafka, the intricate theological or judicial mockery is replaced by moral outrage and bewilderment. What Costello is seeking at the wall and the gate is not the law, as in Kafka's parable, but a defence of fiction, an answer to her sister's condemnation of the novel. Who needs fiction, and why? Instead of merely being told that she can't enter through the gate, as Kafka's man from the country is, Costello is told that she can't enter until she has prepared a statement of what she believes. She prepares two. In one she says that she doesn't believe any-thing – as a novelist. Because believing is not what novelists do; it's just what they don't do. 'I have beliefs,' she says when she is interrogated, 'but I do not believe in them.' This doesn't go down too well. In the second statement she says that she believes in a set of Australian frogs and their annual survival of winter. One of her judges paraphrases her response: 'These Australian frogs of yours embody the spirit of life, which is what you as a storyteller believe in.'[31] Costello thinks this is vapid, but doesn't argue. Does she pass through the gate? We don't know. At the end of the chapter she is still waiting.

In parables, or when we read its stories as parables, literature takes us beyond interpretation, because parables require something more than interpretation. They ask of us not so much immediate action as a scene of application, a place in our lives where their analogies can come home as a form of the literal. We can't make sense of them if we don't

[31] Ibid., pp. 200, 219.

find this scene, if we don't apply them somewhere, if we don't find a connection for them in the world we inhabit. In the different worlds we inhabit. There aren't, as it is often said there are, as many worlds and interpretations as there are readers. That is to overestimate our originality. We are surely not as different from each other as we like to think. But there are differences, and this is the charm and the power of well-angled obliquity. I think it is worth wondering whether the literature that we care about doesn't always work in some way as a parable, since we so often find ourselves wanting to apply it and not just interpret it. In this light, literature becomes intensely, perhaps embarrassingly useful, but it doesn't dictate to us the particular use we make of it. That choice is ours. The choice is important, but it's also good to have still lingering in our minds, as Empson says we do, the way we would have preserved our self-respect if we had chosen differently. Or as we could also say, the stories we might tell if we were not telling ourselves this one.

CHAPTER 5

Missing dates

I

I have thought of this book (and I thought of the original lectures) as telling an optimistic story, but I do see that appearances are against me. It may have seemed that after the bleakness and violence of my Kafka chapter there was nowhere to go but up. Yet a certain gloomy consistency remains among my topics, even when I'm evoking splendid literary instances. Death, suffering, unemployment and hell in my previous chapter; waste and loss in this one; and Nietzsche's madness in the next. I persist in believing the story is not all bad, but obviously I'm going to have to work at persuading my readers.

It's true that thoughts of the dead have been in my mind as I have been writing, and especially of the people named in my dedication: F. W. Dupee because of his work on James and his lessons in irony, J. P. Stern because of his writing on Kafka and my memories of Cambridge, Edward Said because of his recent departure and our closeness in age and other things, and my father because of the constant example he didn't even know he was giving. But thoughts of the dead are not thoughts of death, and once we have made room for the necessary sorrow, it is possible to see how urgently such memories and models invite us to continue in their train.

One of the slightly disturbing pleasures of reading the casual remarks that poets make about poetry – especially English poets in the first half of the twentieth century – is the encounter with their sheer, unapologetic bluntness. It's not just that they don't talk like academic critics or scholars – they don't talk like critics at all. Well, they scarcely talk like people who think much, or pay much attention to their actual topic. Auden is said to have argued that Yeats was 'lying' in 'Sailing to Byzantium' because nobody wants to be a mechanical bird.[1] You remember that Yeats had said:

> Once out of nature I shall never take
> My bodily form from any natural thing,
> But such a form as Grecian goldsmiths make
> Of hammered gold and gold enamelling
> To keep a drowsy Emperor awake;
> Or set upon a golden bough to sing
> To lords and ladies of Byzantium
> Of what is past, or passing, or to come.[2]

How could he be lying? Let's forget, for the moment, all the terminological niceties we have learnt, everything we know about artifice and irony, and the whole much-canvassed question of who is speaking when a poet says I. Even if this really is the one and only W. B. Yeats himself, and even if he actually believes he can get 'out of nature', presumably he still doesn't think he would have an entirely free choice of possibilities for his next avatar. This is a fantasy, a game, an

---

[1] Here is Empson's jaunty version of the same accusation: 'he had said in lines of delicious and haunting beauty that he had chosen never to be reborn as any live thing, only as a cuckoo-clock or thereabouts'. Empson, *Using Biography*. London: Chatto & Windus, 1984, p. 174.

[2] W. B. Yeats, *Collected Poems*. Edited by Richard V. Finneran. Basingstoke: Macmillan, 1989, p. 194

imaginary wish, and the poem makes Sidney's case perfectly: the poet is not affirming, and can't be lying.

Even so, Auden may have been on to something, and we should always be wary when clever people are blunt. Auden was suggesting, I take it, that there was something false about the fantasy as a fantasy; that it represented a longing Yeats didn't really have, couldn't really have. Auden was fond of this kind of distinction, and used it in relation to himself and his writing. 'A dishonest poem is one which expresses, no matter how well, feelings or beliefs which its author never felt or entertained.' He withdrew his poem 'Spain' from later editions of his works not only because it propounded what he felt was a 'wicked doctrine', namely that might is right, but because he himself, he claimed, never held the doctrine; he offered it because it 'sounded to me rhetorically effective' at the time.[3] I think Auden was wrong about the doctrine, or at least wrong in thinking that his poem propounded the doctrine. The poem only proposed that

> History to the defeated
> May say alas but cannot help nor pardon.

It's not clear to me that history has ever even said alas, but I don't think this means that might is right, only that victories and defeats are what they are. Auden may have been wrong about himself, too – I suspect he was telling us that he couldn't bear the thought of actually having held the doctrine he thought was so wicked. But he was half-right about Yeats. 'Sailing to Byzantium', whatever Yeats himself felt about his options for the afterlife, makes the fantasy about the golden

---

[3] W. H. Auden, *Collected Poems*. London: Faber & Faber, 1991, pp. xxv, xxvi.

bird seem rather thin and desperate, an elegant but trivial vocation for a person who has said, in the same poem, that 'soul' should 'sing, and louder sing/For every tatter in its mortal dress'. This thinness becomes part of what makes the poem so moving; not dishonesty but a sort of disarray. But my general point, and the reason for raising this example, is to suggest a way of reading bluntness. We don't have to be oversubtle, but we don't have to take it at its most basic word.

Empson wrote his poem 'Missing Dates' in February 1937, and gave it to John Hayward by way of apology for what he called his 'drunken triviality' (I take this detail, and many more, from John Haffenden's excellent edition of Empson's poems). Empson also told Hayward that 'The name of the thing had better be Villanelle but it is called Missing Dates.'[4] Haffenden says that this is a joke borrowed from *Alice Through the Looking Glass*, where there is a lot of play with the differences among what the name of a song is, what the song is called, and what the name of the song is called – three different things, according to the White Knight. The distinction in Empson's case is pretty obscure, because it's hard to tell what 'had better be' is hinting at. Hayward took 'the name of the thing' to be the label that counted, and passed the poem on to Eliot, who printed it as 'Villanelle' in *The Criterion* in July 1937. Empson himself, when he published the poem in a volume, called it 'Missing Dates'. Perhaps he had abandoned his interest in what its name was, or what its name was called. There are two other villanelles in Empson's *Complete*

[4] William Empson, *The Complete Poems*. Edited by John Haffenden. London: Penguin, 2001, p. 344. Further quotations are from this edition and are indicated in brackets on the page.

Poems (and a couple of near-villanelles too), one of them
('It is the pain, it is the pain, endures') called 'Villanelle'.

In an undated but clearly much later note Empson wrote:
'I need to explain that this poem tells a lie. It says that we
only get old because we are untidy whereas of course the
very tidiest people in their city offices get old too. How it can
be a good poem if it is all wrong I cannot say' [345]. He can't
say. This is the author of *Seven Types of Ambiguity*, and we
might well think there is scarcely anything he can't say.
Empson's strategy with his own poem is exactly the same
as Auden's strategy with Yeats. Misstate the gist or theme of
the poem or the metaphor in the broadest, most reductive
way, and then say it's wrong. There is still another twist,
since Empson is also pretending not to know several things
he knows perfectly well: that many good, even great poems
are 'all wrong' in crucial ways – think of Pound's *Cantos*; that
because of the obliquity in literature that Empson himself did
so much to bring back to our minds, there is a sense in which
a poem can't be wrong or right; and that even if a poem can
be wrong or right, it seems likely that this poem, if you are
not determined to turn your summary into a travesty it, is
not all wrong anyway. What is Empson up to?

Well, first of all he is not asking himself if the poem is a
good one: he is saying it is, but he doesn't know how this can
be. On another occasion he said that it was perhaps his 'best
poem', and that he didn't think 'it's bad because it's untrue'.
He did think that it and his other villanelles sounded 'stiff and
rather like tombstones', but that was an effect he was after.
He was surprised 'but relieved' when I. A. Richards told him
that it was a good comic poem, and he remembered a story
about Kafka reading the opening pages of *The Trial* to his
friends. 'They were all in fits of laughter.' 'If *The Trial* is
funny,' Empson said, 'I'm very willing to believe that my little

poem is funny too ... but it's fairly remote, I should say'
[345–346]. Does he mean that the poem is remote, or the
chance of its being funny is remote?

Both propositions are true, I think, and help us to see what
Empson meant when he said the poem told a lie. He wanted us
to see the difference between what the poem seems to say and
how it seems to work. He was thinking like a critic even if he
was talking like a bruiser. Or to use language less loaded with
guesses about Empson's intentions and more suited to the theme
of this book, we can read the language of his blunt denials and
assertions as a precise pointer to the gap between what the poem
says and what the poem knows. But let's look at the poem.

II

Slowly the poison the whole blood stream fills.
It is not the effort nor the failure tires.
The waste remains, the waste remains and kills.

It is not your system or clear sight that mills
Down small to the consequence a life requires;
Slowly the poison the whole blood stream fills.

They bled an old dog dry yet the exchange rills
Of young dog blood gave but a month's desires
The waste remains, the waste remains and kills.

It is the Chinese tombs and the slag hills
Usurp the soil, and not the soil retires.
Slowly the poison the whole blood stream fills.

Not to have fire is to be a skin that shrills.
The complete fire is death. From partial fires
The waste remains, the waste remains and kills.

It is the poems you have lost, the ills
From missing dates, at which the heart expires.

Slowly the poison the whole blood stream fills.
The waste remains, the waste remains and kills. [79]

'The difficulty of writing a villanelle', Empson said, 'is to stop
it from dying as it goes on. It's very hard to read properly to
justify the form.' And again: 'The only difficulty here is in
reading it properly; the repeated lines ought to mean something different each time' [345]. Let's pause over the structure
of the villanelle, and the curious idea of justifying a form.

The villanelle is an ancient form of European popular
song, which received its modern canonical form in a famous
French poem by Jean Passerat (1534–1602), which begins:

> *J'ai perdu ma tourterelle.*
> *Est-ce point celle que j'oy?*
> *Je veus aller après elle.*

> I have lost my turtle-dove
> Is that not her I hear?
> I wish to go where she is.

And ends:

> *En ne voyant plus la belle*
> *Plus rien de beau je ne voy:*
> *Je veus aller après elle.*

> *Mort, que tant de fois j'appelle,*
> *Pren ce qui se donne à toy:*
> *J'ay perdu ma tourterelle,*
> *Je veus aller après elle.*

> No longer seeing my beauty
> I no longer see any thing beautiful:
> I wish to go where she is.

> Death, whom I call so many times,
> Take what is given to you:

I have lost my turtle-dove,
I wish to go where she is.[5]

The poem – this poem and all the villanelles that came after
it – has 19 lines, composed of five tercets and a quatrain. The
first and the third lines of the poem are repeated in alternat-
ing stanzas, and come together as a couplet at the end. There
are only two rhymes throughout. This sounds a little complicated, and is fiendishly difficult to pull off without sounding like a parrot or a piece of clockwork, but it's easy to see
the pattern once you look at a poem on a page. Empson
thought the poets of his generation were mainly prompted by
the languid villanelle which Stephen Daedalus writes in *A
Portrait of the Artist as a Young Man* (and which Joyce
himself had written long before he thought of Stephen),
but there were other well-known models by Wilde and
Dowson. Hopkins indeed had been very scornful about the
mid-nineteenth century vogue for such forms, and wrote to
Bridges dismissively about 'Gosse, Dobson, and Co' and
their 'fumbling with triolets, villanelles and what not'.[6]
Sylvia Plath wrote some wonderful villanelles, and the
most famous modern ones are perhaps Auden's 'Time will
say nothing but I told you so', and Dylan Thomas's 'Do not
go gentle into that good night'.

My suggestion in this chapter is that if literature knows
something, or knows of something, then we shall need at

[5] Jean Passerat, *Les Poésies françaises*. Paris: A. Lemerre, 1880, 2 vols.,
vol. II, p. 83. My translation.

[6] See Manfred Pfister, 'Die Villanelle in der englischen Moderne'. *Archiv
für das Studium der neueren Sprachen und Literaturen*, vol. 219, no. 2, 1982,
p. 297. And Ronald E. McFarland, *The Villanelle: Evolution of a Poetic
Form*. Moscow, Idaho: University of Idaho Press, 1987, passim.

some stage to ask what literary forms know or know of. I'm hoping that the villanelle will stand in for other forms, and for a whole set of formal questions too baggy for this occasion. My hunch is that the villanelle may well know quite a lot about things like love, loss, repetition, design, language, memory, longing. It's worth remembering that the slight, elegant poem which establishes the form in its modern shape is about loss: '*J'ai perdu ma tourterelle*' ('I have lost my turtledove'). Worth remembering, too, that the light music and returning rhymes of that poem tell a story that can hardly be about loss, or only about loss. I don't think we can study form, in the villanelle or anywhere else, in isolation from the other elements of a work, and especially the semantic ones, what the work says or seems to say. But I do think you can get extraordinary effects by playing form against meaning, and I remember my excitement when I first realized how good these effects can get. I was listening to a radio programme about the collaboration of Bertolt Brecht and Kurt Weill, and the speaker – I wish I could remember who it was – pointed out that Weill had set one of Brecht's sourest and most bitter lyrics to a fabulous lilting melody, one of the most beautiful tunes Weill ever wrote. The lyric – it's from *Mahagonny* – has lines like:

> *Denn wie man sich bettet so liegt man*
> *Es deckt einen keiner da zu*

> For the bed you make is the bed you're going to lie in
> No one's going to tuck you in

And

> *Wenn einer tritt dann bin ich es*
> *Und wird einer getreten dann bist du's.*

> If anyone's doing the kicking its me
> And if anyone gets kicked it's you.[7]

The melodic line sings on as if it had nothing to do with such sentiments. The result is to make the harshness seem nastier, but also a little comic – as if the tough guy, or tough girl in this case, was not so much tough as working hard at being tough.

The villanelle, I think, will always deny the loss it sings of – or rather not deny it, but complicate whatever proposition is being made about it. And the music of Empson's poem, I think, does something of what he thought laughter might have been doing, if anyone apart from Richards had been laughing. What 'justifies' the form is what couldn't happen without it.

III

The poem probably needs a bit of basic glossing before we go any further. 'The waste remains, the waste remains and kills' is an echo, even a parody, of 'The woods decay, the woods decay and fall' from 'Tithonus', which Empson thought was the 'best and deepest' of Tennyson's poems. He called it, as I mentioned in the previous chapter, 'a poem in favour of the human practice of dying'. Empson had read of an experiment in which an old dog was given a young dog's blood. In the account that John Haffenden has unearthed, the old dog does pretty well out of the exchange. 'He ran and barked, a thing he had not done for years ... His coat started to come in ... he was no longer indifferent to the charms of the other sex' [349].

---

[7] Bertolt Brecht and Kurt Weill, *Mahagonny*. Königsdorf: Delta Music Company, 1988. My translation.

Perhaps Empson read a different account, but in any case this cheerful creature doesn't suit his purpose. His old dog gets only a month's desires, and we are not told what he is able to do about them. In a note to his *Collected Poems*, Empson says that 'the legend that a fifth or some such part of the soil of China is given up to ancestral tombs is ... not true' [344]. The point of the analogy is clear, though: the soil is not retreating or diminishing, it is being taken over by death and waste. Empson says elsewhere that he 'always thought "missing dates" was American slang; but it's not American slang, it means failing to come to an appointment' [345]. This is a little odd, since that is just what the American slang means – it merely specializes the nature of the missed appointment a little. The reading of the phrase 'missing dates' that seems to me most appealing is the most literal, the days of the year that have just gone without a trace, holes in the calendar, time lost and not to be regained.

I should also say something about the syntactical trick that Empson likes so much, and uses constantly in his poems: the elision of 'that' or 'which' in sentences which seem to require at least one of them. I assume this usage was once quite frequent, but it seems rare now, even archaic, even obscure. Still, you have only to fill out such sentences to their full grammatical form to see why Empson would like the short version, and why the short version serves his poems so well. 'It is not the effort or the failure that tires ... ' 'It is the Chinese tombs ... that usurp the soil ... ' Not nearly as good as the gnomic lines we have. Of course, Empson uses the long form as well, even here, when he needs it for his rhythm. 'It is not your system or clear sight that mills ... ', 'It is the poems you have lost ... at which the heart expires.' Listed this way, the repetitions of 'It is' reveal their awkwardness and their insistence, and suggest a nagging need not so much to preach as to get the problem to stay in place, to nail it down before it slips away again. 'Much of the verse', Empson said about a late edition of his *Collected Poems*, 'is about the strangeness of the world, in which we are often tripped up and made helpless' [114].

The poison fills the blood stream, and the waste remains and kills. These seem to be two different tracks to death, and each appears to rest on a different argument: invasion or accumulation. We don't know where the poison comes from or why the waste cannot be evacuated, although we are given negative clues. It's not a matter of effort or failure, or of system or clear sight. The third and fourth tercets develop the double proposition through analogy, although the arguments now cross over. You can perhaps, like the dog, have your poisoned blood changed for a new complement, but you will get only a brief respite, not a fresh start. The conclusion of this thought, however, mentions waste rather than poison. The example of the Chinese tombs suggests that there is no point in getting rid of old waste if new waste is rising all the time. It is death that is rising, of course, but the slag hills look more like waste. The conclusion here, continuing the crossover, names poison.

The tercet about fire takes a different, three-way tack. The shrilling skin, Mary Jacobus brilliantly suggested in conversation, is an allusion to Marsyas, a flute-playing centaur who recklessly agreed to take part in a musical contest against Apollo. There was no doubt about the verdict but the god turned out to be what we might call a sore winner, since he had Marsyas flayed alive and nailed his skin to a pine – 'or, some say, to a plane-tree', Robert Graves adds.[8] The shrilling skin is defeated and tortured music, we might say. It avoids both

[8] Robert Graves, *The Greek Myths*. Harmondsworth: Penguin, 1960, 2 vols., vol. I, p. 77.

poison and waste, but at what cost? 'The complete fire' also avoids these things, and life itself as well. 'Partial fires' take us back to where we were, the world of lingering waste.

As we arrive at the quatrain we have in our minds: effort and failure; system and sight; a transfusion giving only a month's desires; tombs and slag heaps usurping (presumably arable) soil; and a proposition about a relation to fire, all or none or partial. We are more than ready for the meeting of the two tracks of argument at the end of the poem, which the crossovers have announced, and which the very form of the villanelle has always had in store for us. There aren't two tracks, there never were two tracks. Poison and waste are just two names for the same thing. It doesn't matter whether the poison rises or the waste fails to sink. But now the poem seems to leave the figurative mode behind, or at least to offer a clear translation of its figures into direct experience:

> It is the poems you have lost, the ills
> From missing dates, at which the heart expires.
> Slowly the poison the whole blood stream fills.
> The waste remains, the waste remains and kills.

Lost poems, missing dates, these are the things that kill. They are the poison and the waste. But does the poison cause the waste, or is poison a name for regret, a way of making waste worse? Empson's paraphrase, you will remember, alludes to the fate of a particular mentality or character: the messy person's life, which tidiness would avoid. Both poison and waste are figures for getting old, and we all get old. But neither poison nor unremitting waste is an unalterable feature of being alive, and the poem derives all its grim authority from its note of harsh regret, the sense that things could have been otherwise and now will not be. The 'untruth' in the poem, if you like, is its transparent or failed attempt to disguise self-laceration as an aspect of the unchanging human condition. 'The refrains', Ezra Pound said, thinking of a villanelle by Ernest Dowson, 'are an emotional fact, which the intellect, in the gyrations of the poem, tries in vain and in vain to escape.'[9] In 'Missing Dates' the emotional fact is rue, and the refrains are a bid to give this condition some kind of intellectual certificate. This interpretation may help us to think about the flat, sad certainty of the pain in the poem, and perhaps give us a way of converting its assertions into something we can recognize more nearly, something that would make its truth truer or its lie more persuasive. We might want to ask how poems get lost, what it means to lose a poem. Or why one misses a date. How one discovers that a date has gone missing.

In his reading of 'Missing Dates', Christopher Ricks pauses over the word consequence – 'the consequence a life requires'. He thinks the poem is not 'clear to itself about the consequence this poem requires', but I would suggest that this lack of clarity may be part of its strange force.[10] I hadn't paused over 'consequence' until I reread Ricks, and then small bells began tinkling in my head. It was a while before I realized they were saying *Macbeth*:

> If it were done when 'tis done, then 'twere well
> It were done quickly. If the assassination
> Could trammel up the consequence, and catch,
> With his surcease, success . . . [11]

[9] Quoted by Pfister in 'Die Villanelle in der englischen Moderne', p. 298.
[10] Christopher Ricks, *The Force of Poetry*. Oxford: Clavendon Press, 1984, p. 239.
[11] William Shakespeare, *Macbeth*. Edited by A. R. Braunmüller. Cambridge: Cambridge University Press, 1997, p. 131.

This is one of the passages Empson writes about most brilliantly in *Seven Types of Ambiguity*. He says, as most editors do, that 'his' could mean his or its, and could refer to Duncan, the assassination or the consequence; and that 'success' means fortunate result, any result, or succession. He says all kinds of other wonderful things as well, and then writes:

And *catch*, the single little flat word among these monsters, names an action; it is a mark of human inadequacy to deal with these matters of statecraft, a child snatching at the moon as she rides thunder-clouds. The meanings cannot all be remembered at once, however often you read them; it remains the incantation of a murderer, dishevelled and fumbling among the powers of darkness.[12]

The speaker of 'Missing Dates' is in a different place, and in spite of the poem's gloom he is not among the powers of darkness in the way Macbeth is. He is probably not a murderer, and indeed such a determined intervention into the course of things seems incompatible with the monotony of his despair. But he is dishevelled and fumbling, and he does want to trammel up the consequence. Or does he? 'Trammel', Empson says, 'was a technical term used about netting birds, hobbling horses in some particular way, hooking up pots, levering, and running trolleys on rails', and the *New Cambridge Shakespeare* adds 'bind up or wrap (a corpse)'. It's not obvious just what it is that is milled 'down small to the consequence a life requires', or indeed what is doing the milling. It seems that life itself is ground down by its own demand for consequence, and that this is another name for the poison that fills up the blood stream. But what is consequence?

[12] William Empson, *Seven Types of Ambiguity*. Norfolk: New Directions, 1966, p. 50.

For Macbeth it is whatever follows from an act, and his desperate fantasy is that the act itself could net or hobble or wrap up its own consequences. There wouldn't be any consequences. Duncan would be dead, and that would be an end of it. For the speaker of 'Missing Dates' consequence must mean the same thing – at least I hope it does, because that is why I was listening to the bells in my head – but the project is different, or rather it also involves wrapping up consequences but with a different implication and affect. Consequence, again, is what follows from action, but in the poem it suggests mere consistency, a form of death. This, I think, is how Empson gets to his paraphrase about the tidy people. They are all consequence and nothing else. There is a logical contradiction here, which is also – from the point of view of the self-punishing speaker – a satisfying double irony. If we ignore consequence, as untidy people do, the waste mounts up and the poison spreads. If we attend to consequence, as tidy people do, the very narrowness of our concentration mills us down. The organized life becomes a waste, rather than a defeat by waste, and has a poison all its own. 'The time must come,' Empson writes of Fielding, 'if a man carries through a consistent programme about double irony, when he himself does not know the answer.'[13]

In *Some Versions of Pastoral*, commenting on Gray's 'Elegy Written in a Country Churchyard', Empson writes: 'it is only in degree that any improvement of society could prevent wastage of human powers; the waste even in a fortunate life, the isolation even of a life rich in intimacy, cannot but be felt deeply, and is the central feeling of tragedy'. Empson is not saying that tragedy, waste and isolation are all there is, but he is saying that they are everywhere: 'even in a

[13] Empson, *Using Biography*, p. 144

fortunate life', 'even ... a life rich in intimacy'. He also writes, elsewhere in the same book, of 'a generous distaste for the conditions of life', and the 'feeling that life is essentially inadequate to the human spirit, and yet that a good life must avoid saying so'.[14] A good life must avoid saying so, but what about a good poem? 'Missing Dates' is all about inadequacy and doesn't seem to be avoiding anything, as long as it's self-accusatory enough. The grand, dark claims of waste and shortfall conjure up the plights I earlier associated with the names of Roland Barthes and J. L. Austin: 'the fundamental inadequation of language and the real', and 'the innumerable and unforeseeable demands of the world upon language'.[15] But neither Barthes nor Austin would write of 'the human spirit', and their engagement is with the performance of words. Empson concentrates on that performance, too, but sees in it an embodiment of the very 'conditions of life'.

But then those conditions, for Empson, are caught up in literary form. A form, as a form, can't enact an essential inadequacy any more than it can proclaim a complete triumph, and it can't rest with an assertion, however powerful, of tragedy and waste and isolation. The very rhyming of 'kills' and 'fills' starts up a counter-movement. I'm not saying that form is always cheerful, like the Kurt Weill waltz, and I don't wish to invoke the gaiety of the Chinamen in Yeats's poem 'Lapis Lazuli' – well, not substantively and not yet:

> All things fall and are built again
> And those that build them again are gay ...

[14] William Empson, *Some Versions of Pastoral*. New York: New Directions, 1974, pp. 5, 114–115.
[15] Roland Barthes *Leçon*. Paris: Editions du Seuil, 1978 p. 22; J. L. Austin, *Sense and Sensibilia*. Edited by G. J. Warnock. Oxford: Oxford University Press, 1964, p. 73.

Their eyes mid many wrinkles, their eyes,
Their ancient, glittering eyes, are gay.[16]

No one is rebuilding anything in Empson's 'Missing Dates'. But the form is doing its work. Its very economy, its sparsity of rhyme, resists the idea of waste; and the repeated lines, as Empson hoped they would, change their meaning with each repetition. And if they change their meaning they can't mean just what they say, or rather they can, but they will say different things each time, and so say four things each, at least. Well, what Empson was suggesting was that one should emphasize a different word with each repetition. It's easy to see what can happen:

> *Slowly* the poison the whole blood stream fills.
> Slowly the *poison* the whole blood stream fills.
> Slowly the poison the *whole* blood stream fills.
> Slowly the poison the whole blood stream *fills*.

Or we could stress 'blood' or 'stream' or either of the definite articles.

More important than these possible shifts of emphasis, however, is a powerful general effect. One of the things the poem begins to suggest, if we concentrate on its dark repetitions, with their gloomy beat, is that there is something swaggering and pompous about these melancholy claims. Philip and Averil Gardner, in their commentary on Empson's poems, *The God Approached*, rather charmingly say that 'As a set of statements about life ... 'Missing Dates' is almost too pessimistic to be true.'[17] It's not too pessimistic

---

[16] Yeats, *Collected Poems*, p. 295.

[17] Philip and Averil Gardner, *The God Approached*. Totowa, N.J.: Rowman and Littlefield, 1978, p. 185.

to be true – what is? – but it may be too pessimistic to be said. Empson would be the first to understand this, and he wouldn't mind us laughing, if we could bring ourselves to laugh. Imagine the lines as spoken by the characters in *Waiting for Godot*.

> Vladimir: Slowly the poison the whole blood stream fills.
>
> Estragon: Too slowly.
>
> Vladimir: Well, at least the waste remains, there's that to say for it.
>
> Estragon: For what?
>
> Vladimir: For life. Or death. The waste remains.
>
> Estragon: And kills. Don't forget the best bit.

IV

Elizabeth Bishop's 'One Art' is a very well-known poem, and I would apologize for discussing such a familiar work if it were not so good. And if my experience didn't suggest that it is simultaneously well known (by some) and not known at all (by everybody else) – there doesn't appear to be any middle ground.

In form it is not quite an orthodox villanelle, since it repeats one full line and one rhyme word, rather than two full lines; and some of its rhymes are off-rhymes: master, fluster, gesture. But it feels like a villanelle, and its refusal of the repetition of the full line takes away some of the threat of heaviness which lurks in the supposedly light form. This is what Auden avoids through tripping rhythms and an epigrammatic cleverness, and Thomas avoids by sheer bravura and eloquence. Empson, I think, doesn't entirely avoid the heaviness, but his poem has other virtues, as we have seen. Our question here, as before, is what does this literary form know? What does it know, as I have already asked, about love, loss, repetition, design, language, memory, longing? My suggestion is that the form, as Bishop uses it, knows a lot about what remains and what returns, like a rhyme, like a line, and a lot about what it means to put your feelings into an order that someone else has used for other feelings. The poem is, as Lloyd Schwartz says, 'one of Elizabeth Bishop's rare excursions into a complex, pre-existent verse pattern (only her two sestinas and the double sonnet of "The Prodigal" come to mind)'.[18] It would be sentimental to use the word 'community' here but a writer who borrows an ancient and established form cannot be alone, and there are times when just not being alone feels like a blessing. The form knows this, and Bishop would like to believe it. She is trying to get a little help from the form.

Here is the poem.

The art of losing isn't hard to master;
so many things seem filled with the intent
to be lost that their loss is no disaster.

Lose something every day. Accept the fluster
of lost door keys, the hour badly spent.
The art of losing isn't hard to master.

Then practice losing farther, losing faster:
places, and names, and where it was you meant
to travel. None of these will bring disaster.

[18] Lloyd Schwartz, 'One Art: The Poetry of Elizabeth Bishop', in *Elizabeth Bishop and Her Art*, ed. Lloyd Schwartz and Sybil Estess. Ann Arbor: University of Michigan Press, 1983, p. 150.

> I lost my mother's watch. And look! my last, or
> next-to-last, of three loved houses went.
> The art of losing isn't hard to master.
>
> I lost two cities, lovely ones. And, vaster,
> some realms I owned, two rivers, a continent.
> I miss them, but it wasn't a disaster.
>
> – Even losing you (the joking voice, a gesture
> I love) I shan't have lied. It's evident
> the art of losing's not too hard to master
> though it may look like (*Write* it!) like disaster.[19]

There is an element of mockery, of dry self-criticism in the idea of owning (and then losing) cities, realms, rivers, a continent, the very grandeur and folly of such claims pointing us towards an awareness of the grandeur and folly of imagining we can own a person. And yet it is possible, painfully possible, to lose what one never possessed. Or to feel as if that is what has happened.

A number of drafts of this poem are held in the Library at Vassar College. They make fascinating reading, and they show Bishop working from a much longer, looser piece towards the closer, tighter poem we have. The first version is far more openly wry and humorous than the last , or it's wry and humorous until it gets to its wrenching ending. It has three possible titles, 'How to Lose Things', 'The Gift of Losing Things' and 'The Art of Losing Things'. It doesn't look anything like a villanelle, but Bishop has written some notes for a rhyme scheme at the bottom of the sheet, and all the later drafts have lists of possible rhymes – a villanelle, you will remember, has only two rhymes, and the structure,

---

[19] Elizabeth Bishop, *The Complete Poems*. New York: Farrar, Strans and Geroux, 1984, p. 178.

allowing for the repetitions, calls for seven rhymes on one sound, and six on another. One of the drafts has almost nothing but rhyme words, including the word 'aster', as in 'eyes of azure aster', which Bishop doesn't get rid of until quite late in the game. So it may be that this first draft is a verse paraphrase or outline of the poem she planned to structure quite differently, rather an than early form of the poem itself. Whatever it is, it's extraordinarily instructive.[20]

In this version the poet pretends to take us fully into her confidence. 'I really want to introduce *myself* – I am . . . fantastically good at losing things/I think everyone should profit from my experiences.'

> You may find it hard to believe, but I have actually lost
> I mean *lost*, and forever, two whole houses,
> one a very big one.

The list continues – it contains a peninsula and an island, a small-sized town, a beach, a bay, 'two of the world's biggest cities', and a piece of a continent – and then the poet makes the move we now see she was leading up to all the time:

> One might think this would have prepared me
> for losing one average-sized, not exceptionally
> beautiful or dazzlingly intelligent person
> (only the eyes *were* exceptionally beautiful and the hands *looked*
> intelligent)
> But it doesn't seem to have, at all . . .

[20] There is an excellent account of the drafts of the poem in Brett C. Millier, *Elizabeth Bishop: Life and the Memory of It*. Berkeley: University of California Press, 1993, pp. 508–513. I have taken my quotations from these pages.

The draft ends:

> He who loseth his life etc. – but he who
> loses his love – never, no never never never again –

The poet is keeping the disaster at a distance through the mockery of her own skill at losing things, and almost to the end registers the pain of loss through determined under-statement: 'one might think', 'doesn't seem to have'. The understatement makes the pain of loss all the clearer, of course. The loss is literal, and irredeemable, and later drafts make this fact more obvious still:

> All that I write is false, it's evident
> The art of losing isn't hard to master.
> oh no.
> anything at all anything but one's love. (Say it: disaster.)

In other drafts Bishop insists again and again on the untruth of her own central claim – 'I'm writing lies now', 'I wrote a lot of lies'. And then suddenly she switches. 'All lies now' becomes 'not lies', and 'All that I write is false' becomes 'doesn't mean I've lied'. 'And losing you now ... doesn't mean I've lied.' 'In losing you I haven't lied above.' What has happened?

Well, a wonderful Empsonian ambiguity has arisen. 'I haven't lied' seems to cancel 'I wrote a lot of lies', and certainly this is the basic meaning of the verbal gesture. I said that the art of losing isn't hard to master but I was lying. Now I'm saying that I wasn't lying when I said the art of losing isn't hard to master. But of course there aren't any such simple cancellations in matters of any human import-ance, and the denial of the lie contains the lie it seeks to put

aside. This would be true even if we hadn't been following the
trail of this particular claim. 'And losing you now ... doesn't
mean I've lied.' You wouldn't say you weren't lying unless
there was at least a possibility that you might be.

Still, the denial does alter the poem completely, and shifts
its pathos to a quite different ground. A story about the
ability to master all losses but one becomes a story about how
all losses both can and cannot be mastered – everything
depends on what sort of mastery you will settle for, and
whether mastery is what you want. With this we can turn
back to the poem as Bishop published it, in the volume
Geography III, in 1976.

V

We pass readily – too readily, I want to suggest, as Bishop's
own logic did in her early drafts – over the first, literal level of
meaning in the poem: the claim that the art of losing is not
hard to master, that loss doesn't have to be a disaster. We
think we know better than that, and our first move is to invert
the meaning: the art cannot be mastered, disaster is the final
and only word. But perhaps the second, apparently sophisticated move is in its way just as naive as the first. Just what is it
we think we know? That it isn't easy to lose things, and that a
clever modern poet can't be telling us it is. We know an irony
when we see one. But to read in this way – to read too quickly –
is to underestimate the poem in its final version, and to fail to
hear what it is saying on the simplest plane. The poem is not
saying that bearing loss is easy, only that loss is easily come by.
Well, it is saying a lot about bearing loss, too, but the humdrum
truth is important. It is easy to lose keys, time, watches, people.
Scarcely an art at all. We do it all the time. The irony here
would be in Bishop's pretending it is an art.

There are plenty of other ironies, of course, or gaps between what the words of the poem say and what they are doing. The rhetorical mode of the poem is that of an apparent prescription, an instruction, which is really a performance; a proposed relation to memory which seeks to enact that relation in the present. When Bishop tells herself, in italics and with an exclamation mark, to '*Write* it!', she is trying to get to the end of the actual sentence she is writing (or to mime such a motion) and to arrive one more time at the repeated word disaster. The art of losing, difficult or not to master, includes the art of writing, perhaps consists of the art of writing.[21] What does it mean to call this art, of losing and/or writing, 'one art', as the title of the poem does? Is it one art among many? The one art we need? Or is the title more sardonic than that, is the suggestion perhaps that losing is not an art at all, that it is sheer madness to think of loss in this way, and only a writer would even try it? Proust's narrator discovered that he could regain time because he hadn't really lost it. But what if he really had?

The other obvious performative moment in the poem, which happens once for the writer and the speaker, but happens time and again for every re-reader, is the slight shift from 'isn't hard' to 'not too hard'. On several occasions when I have copied the poem out I have missed the change, automatically typed 'isn't hard', as if I thought the poem kept saying just that. The shift is slight, but real, and I find it impossible to talk about it without either overplaying

---

[21] 'The poem toys with the formal control that might make losing, not just a way of life, but also a way of art. What happens, however, is that the two things come apart. By the last stanza, the form, with its hammered rhyme, loses everything except itself.' Angela Leighton, 'Elegies of Form in Bishop, Plath, Stevenson'. *Proceedings of the British Academy*, vol. 121, 2002.

it or underplaying it. How could such a shift not matter?
How could it matter as much as I am going to make it
matter once I've pointed it out? An excellent instance of
Bishop's discretion and difficulty. When I read her I feel
I'm reading her, Elizabeth Bishop and none other. When I
talk about her I feel I'm talking about someone else, some
more voluble, intelligible figure I keep inventing. But
here's what I can do.

What changes when the idiom changes, I think, when we
move from 'isn't hard' to 'not too hard', is not the meaning
but what J. L. Austin would call the force of the utterance.
Not hard and not too hard are too close for the difference to
carry any great semantic weight – or rather we can get them
to carry such a weight only by the kind of clumsy emphasis
that Bishop is beautifully avoiding. Not *too* hard, we might
say, with loud italics. But the only italics in the poem itself
are not there. 'Not too hard', without the italics, makes clear
that the previous phrase 'isn't hard' was not a declarative but
also, in its turn, a performative action, the expression of a
wish or fiction, the naming of a desired relation between
possession and loss. But it was a fiction rather than a complete fantasy or piece of self-delusion. 'Isn't hard' has among
its meanings: one day perhaps it won't be as hard as it is now.
And 'not too hard', apart from revealing this sense – or
rather confirming it, since we have suspected its presence
from the beginning of the poem – suggests three quite
different and contradictory possibilities of interpretation.

One is the darker possibility I think most of us tend to
glide towards: the art of losing's not too hard to master, it is
impossible to master, its only option is to become an art of
naming disaster. Still an art, and not just an inversion of the
literal meaning of the poem, but a sorry art, and an abolition
of the very chance that much of the poem's irony seems to be

trying to keep alive. Through her mixture of instruction and memory ('lose', 'practice'; 'I lost', 'I lost'), Bishop would be seeking both to lose time as it passes, and to recall old times in order to see how lost they are. The practice of losing would be a sort of endlessly failed protection against the fact of loss.

Then there is the more gradual, but perhaps even sadder reading that creeps up on us as we return to the poem, and the poem's idea of returning. There is one thing worse than failing to master loss, and that is succeeding in mastering it. We cannot bear to become, or to think of becoming, the person who will no longer feel what is harrowing us now. Proust's narrator writes of 'the slow, agonizing suicide of the self which loved Gilberte'. 'The only thing I cared for, my relationship with Gilberte, was the very thing I was trying to sabotage ... through my gradual fostering not of her indif-ference towards me, but – which would come to the same thing in the end – of mine towards her.'[22]

The third possibility is that there is something wrong with the notion of loss, as I think the poem has delicately, humorously been trying to tell us all along. The feeling of loss is all too real, and so is the feeling of disaster. But we can be right about our feelings and wrong about the grounds for them, and the poem teaches us, I think, the rudiments of an art quite different from the art of losing, and indeed quite different from any art of mastery.

The key phrase here is 'I shan't have lied', Bishop's last revision of her sentence about lying – in an almost-final draft

---

[22] Marcel Proust, *A la recherche du temps perdu*. Paris: Gallimard, 1987–1989, 4 vols., vol. I, p. 600. *In the Shadow of Young Girls in Flower*. Translated by James Grieve. London: Penguin, 2002, pp. 186–187.

she was writing 'these are not lies', 'I still don't lie' – and in it
resides everything I have said so far, and much more. These
propositions, for instance. That loss can perhaps be mastered,
even if not now. That loss can't be mastered but our longing
for such mastery is irresistible. That loss can't be mastered but
it's important for one's psychic survival to pretend that it can.
None of these propositions is a lie, or has to be a lie. But then 'I
shan't have lied' also suggests a rather different truth, which
we could parse in this way. 'I shall lose you, I shall say it's not
a disaster, and I shan't be lying. Of course, I shall be lying in
the deepest and most obvious way: it will be the worst disaster
of my life. But in another sense I shall be telling a simple truth.
Because we both know we can't lose what was never ours, and
we have always suspected that the whole nomenclature of
these emotions is amiss.'

The poem is suggesting, I think, that we need to refuse the
notion of possession and question the notion of loss. That we
need to try to see vanishing as something other than loss, as
Rilke also invites us to. To learn how to talk of our condition
in something other than spooked or religious terms, invok-
ing ghosts or redemption or forfeited paradises. Wouldn't
there be an ordinary, uneconomic form of vanishing that
wasn't loss at all, and wouldn't there be all kinds of ordinary
ways in which what vanishes may remain? In memory, for
example, but also in the active pursuit of what vanished
objects and persons continue to mean to us.

'All losses haunt us', Empson writes in a poem called
'Success'. This is a story we often tell and often want to
hear and it is true that many losses haunt us. It is truer,
though, I think, that we are haunted, and like to give the
name of loss to our haunting. Empson's next words provide
an extraordinary impetus to a rethinking of all grand
melancholies:

All losses haunt us. It was a reprieve
Made Dostoevsky talk out queer and clear.[23]

What Dostoevsky lost was his death by firing squad, since he was pardoned at the last minute, along with a group of other political prisoners. The whole thing had been a cruel sham, meant to be a lesson. What he gained was the experience of the sham itself, and his life. Once you pause over it, it's hard to see this as a story of loss in any intelligible sense, easy to see how haunting the experience would be, and how it could induce you to talk out queer and clear.

The movement is similar in Bishop's poem, only she uses an elegant false parallelism where Empson uses a kind of non sequitur. After a wry, self-mocking list of things we can and do lose (keys, time, names, plans, a watch, houses), Bishop moves to a set of things we can't lose (cities, rivers, a continent, the voice and gestures of a loved person), and the readings I have proposed of 'not too hard' depend on what we do with this parallelism. If we accept it as metaphorically true, false only in a boring literal sense – we can't really lose rivers, we can't lose what we can't possess – we have our desperate but in the end deeply satisfying story of loss. All losses haunt us, the art of losing is an art of disaster – even if we master it, and especially if we master it. If we read the metaphor of such comprehensive loss as a (beautiful) temptation to pathos but not the end of the story, then we have to ask just what it is that happens when we feel ourselves bereft of loved places or persons; if loss is the right term for our condition; if the tale of loss is the only tale we should be trying to tell.

---

[23] Empson, *The Complete Poems*, p. 80.

'*Les vrais paradis sont les paradis qu'on a perdus.*' ('The true paradises are the paradises we have lost.')[24] Proust almost certainly means paradises are real, but not real until they are lost; are not paradises until they are lost. I have always wanted him to mean that paradises are created by loss, that they are nothing other than our most spectacular name for loss. That loss itself, real enough in many circumstances, is a mystification in others. The story of loss is the narrative form we give to a simpler, more desolate condition: the absence from our side of a loved person, the sense that we shall never again see loved cities and landscapes. As if to miss people and places was always and only to have lost them; as if mortality itself, time in its most banal and irredeemable aspect, was not a fact but a lapse, an error in someone's accounting, a missing date. There is a vast consolation in such a view, but perhaps we could do better than console ourselves, and I think Bishop's poem, and the form of her poem, are suggesting we can.

[24] Proust, *A la recherche de temps perdu*, vol. IV, p. 449. *Finding Time Again.* Translated by Ian Patterson. London: Penguin, 2002, p. 179.

CHAPTER 6

The fictionable world

I

'The fictionable world' is a phrase from *Finnegans Wake*, and the pun is obvious. Joyce is thinking of the fashionable world, and putting himself at some distance from it. But the idea that a world could be fictionable, as a slander or an insult, say, may be actionable, does perhaps have some force to it. There would, for the word to make sense, have to be worlds which are not fictionable, and we could wonder what they are. And then fictionable wouldn't mean quite the same as fictional, or fictitious. It would mean available for conversion into fiction; ripe or ready for fiction, or at least not intrinsically resistant to it. A fictionable world would perhaps catch fiction's eye; fiction would find it promising. Fiction might even start a fashion.

This chapter falls into two parts: one about a string of reactions to the story of Nietzsche's lapse into madness, and one about a recent novel which revisits the scene of that madness. The underlying question in both cases is what Nietzsche called '*le gai savoir*', or '*la gaya scienza*' – the title of his famous book is *Die Fröhliche Wissenschaft*, ordinarily translated as *The Gay Science*. Bernard Williams's introduction to a recent English-language edition glosses this phrase gracefully and amply:

The word 'Wissenschaft' ... means any organized study or body of knowledge, including history, philology, criticism and generally what we call 'the humanities', and that is often what Nietzsche has in mind when he uses the word ... But in the title itself there is an idea still broader than this. It translates a phrase, 'gai saber' ... which referred to the art of song cultivated by the medieval troubadours of Provence ... and it invokes an aristocratic culture of courtly love ... But the title has other implications as well. One ... is that ... Nietzsche's 'gay science' does not in the first place consist of a doctrine, a theory or body of knowledge. While it involves and encourages hard and rigorous thought, and to this extent the standard implications of 'Wissenschaft' are in place, it is meant to convey a certain spirit, one that in relation to understanding and criticism could defy the 'spirit of gravity'.[1]

Both parts of this chapter are an enquiry into whether this spirit can in fact be defied, and what the implications of success or failure are for the relations between literature and knowledge; for our knowledge of what literature knows, or knows of.

II

One of the interesting features of a fictionable world would be that it would be hard to know what stage it was at when we met it – how much fictioning, so to speak, had already taken place. We could in theory meet it as raw fact, just about ready for fiction, but untouched by it. This seems unlikely, though. There are plenty of hard facts in the historical world, like death and bombing and the unrepealable orders of certain politicians, but even they are surrounded by fictions, have fictions behind them or inside

---

[1] Bernard Williams, 'Introduction', Nietzsche, *The Gay Science*. Cambridge: Cambridge University Press, 2001, pp. x–xi.

them. I'm not suggesting that everything is fiction or that there are no facts. Even Nietzsche didn't say that, although he is regularly supposed to have. Well, he did say it, but it wasn't all he said. His remark in its context goes like this: 'Against positivism, which insists on the phenomenon that there are only facts, I would say: no, facts are just what there are not, there are only interpretations.'[2]

And against a philosophy which insisted that there are only interpretations, Nietzsche would no doubt have had something to say in favour of the facts. Even if we take the radically sceptical position that there are no facts that are not already thoroughly infiltrated by interpretation, we don't get rid of the facts. The facts become what we call the stage of interpretation before the one we are at now, just as Rousseau, according to Paul de Man, 'calls natural any stage of relational integration that precedes in degree the stage presently under examination'.[3]

But then what are 'the facts'? We could see them not just as tangible objects or unavoidable edicts, but as the way things are, provisionally or not. However they are wherever you are. Or however *they* are wherever *you* are. The facts in this sense would be what Henry James called the real: what we cannot possibly not know, like the fact that I can't walk through the wall, but also the fact that the person I have been relentlessly pursuing with my affection really doesn't love me, and that racial prejudice is not an invention of the liberal press. Wittgenstein has a wonderful exchange on this subject, and I mentioned its key phrase, *'wie es sich verhält'*,

[2] Friedrich Nietzsche, *Werke* Edited by Karl Schlechta. Munich: Hanser, 1966, 3 vols; vol. III, p. 903. My translation.
[3] Paul de Man, *Allegories of Reading*. New Haven: Yale University Press, 1979, p. 249.

translated by G. E. M. Anscombe as 'the facts', in an earlier chapter. 'Exchange' is a manner of speaking. Wittgenstein is talking to himself. He is arguing that words, in this case names, have meanings but not fixed meanings – a little later, he italicizes fixed:

> By 'Moses' I understand the man who did what the Bible relates of Moses, or at any rate a good deal of it. But how much? Have I decided how much must be proved false for me to give up my proposition as false? Has the name 'Moses' got a fixed and unequivocal use for me in all possible cases?

The answer is no, and Wittgenstein tells us, in a rather unlikely domestic analogy, that a table can still be useful even if it wobbles. Then he says:

> Should it be said that I am using a word whose meaning I don't know, and so am talking nonsense? – Say what you choose, so long as it does not prevent you from seeing the facts. (And when you see them there is a good deal that you will not say.) (*Soll man sagen, ich gebrauche ein Wort, dessen Bedeutung ich nicht kenne, rede also Unsinn? – Sage, was du willst, solange dich das nicht verhindert, zu sehen, wie es sich verhält. [Und wenn du das siehst, wirst du Manches nicht sagen.]*)[4]

It is important to see the facts, and to listen to their rather daunting invitation to silence. But there is a lot to be said about the unmarked traffic between fact and fiction. For instance, how deep into fiction are we when we pick up the story of Nietzsche in Turin?. Nietzsche steps out on to the street one day in 1889, 3 January to be precise, and sees a horse being beaten by its

[4] Ludwig Wittgenstein, *Philosophical Investigations*. Translated by G. E. M. Anscombe. Oxford: Blackwell, 1967, p. 37.

driver. Nietzsche throws his arms around the horse's neck, and collapses into what turns out to be terminal madness, although he doesn't die for some years. There are many accounts of this event, and many allusions to it. I want to look briefly at two basic versions, and then explore in detail three variations on it, which we find in a novel by Milan Kundera, an essay by Roland Barthes, and the responses to a lecture by Georges Bataille. The Kundera and the Barthes variations are easily quoted and evoked; brief but very rich. The responses to Bataille, and Bataille's responses to the responses, are going to take a little reconstruction.

But first, how basic are the basic accounts? Here is the standard, most often cited older reconstruction, which is to be found in E. F. Podach's book, *Nietzsches Zusammenbruch*, 1930 (*Nietzsche's Collapse*, or *Nietzsche's Breakdown*):

On the third of January, as Nietzsche is just leaving his house, he sees that at the cab stand on the Piazza Carlo Alberto a tired old nag is being beaten by a brutal driver. Pity (or sympathy: '*Mitleid*') overcomes him. Sobbing and protecting ('*schluchzend und schutzend*') he throws his arms around the neck of the suffering horse. He collapses. Fortunately Fino arrives, drawn by the crowd on the street. He recognizes his lodger and with great difficulty takes him up into the house.[5]

This is fairly plain reporting, but also a good example of how much discreet projection can get into plain talk. The horse is tired and old, and the driver is brutal. As if lively young horses don't get whipped into action by quite ordinary coachmen. But perhaps the horse really was tired and old. It certainly could have been, but how would we know? That's what it's like in the fictionable world. This is an actual, individual horse,

[5] E. F. Podach, *Nietzsches Zusammenbruch*. Heidelberg: Kampmannverlag, 1930, p. 82. My translation, German words Podach's.

and it was either tired and old or not. But we can't be sure its tiredness and age are not Podach's contribution, that they haven't crept into the story as part of the general picture of pity.[6] An eyewitness, or an earwitness, might well report that Nietzsche was sobbing, but only God or a novelist, we might think, could know for sure that it was pity that overcame him, and that his gesture was meant to be protective. In fact, this story is already a full-blown little parable. The pity is there because Nietzsche had attacked it so often. Zarathustra had plenty to say about pity as a vice, and in his own person Nietzsche wrote, 'The suffering of others infects us, pity is an infection.'[7] The parable then is either ironic or defensive. It shows the enemy of pity finally overcome by pity itself; or it suggests that Nietzsche was not a real enemy of pity, or not an enemy of real pity, whatever he might be saying as a philosopher.[8] Podach, I think, leaned to the second view, but there has been no shortage of people to take the first.

Here is another, much more recent account:

On 3 January 1889 or thereabouts [Nietzsche] tearfully embraced a mistreated nag in the street. The horse under duress was pulling a public conveyance on or near the Via Po. It may have fallen first or

---

[6] Janz, who places the event four days later, on 7 January, thinks the projection may have come from Nietzsche rather than Podach. 'The question remains whether a striking instance of mistreatment of an animal really occurred, or whether Nietzsche with his troubled gaze read such cruelty into the situation.' Curt Paul Janz, *Friedrich Nietzsche: Biographie*. Munich: Hanser, 1979, p. 34. My translation.

[7] Friedrich Nietzsche, *The Will to Power*, trans. Walter Kauffman and R. J. Hollingdale. New York: Vintage, 1968, p. 199.

[8] 'We recall the man whose mouthpiece – Zarathustra – considers pity to be his last sin as having, shortly before his collapse, flung his arms in tears around the neck of a cart-horse [*sic*] being maltreated by its owner.' Otto Bohlman, *Yeats and Nietzsche*. London: Macmillan, 1982, p. 5.

he embraced it and then fell himself, briefly losing consciousness. The accounts are various ... [9]

This is cautious to the point of comedy. We don't know for sure when the event happened or on what street, and we don't know whether it was Nietzsche or the horse who fell down first. The sobbing is still there, or at least the tears are; but 'mistreated' and 'duress' seem slightly evasive. Whose view is this, and what exactly was happening to the horse?

It doesn't matter too much to Lesley Chamberlain because for her the action is elsewhere, and earlier. Nietzsche 'had already dreamed the gesture the previous May', she says, 'and written it in a letter'. She thinks it possible, too, that he was remembering a passage in Dostoevsky's *Crime and Punishment*, where a horse is being beaten. 'When Nietzsche dreamed of the mistreated horse he felt pity; he wanted to weep. Now in reality some ultimate autobiographical urge made him embrace a real horse ... '[10] The story is still about pity, and the two readings of the parable are still in place. But the dream is the real scene of pity, and the street in Turin only a belated literalization. I'm not sure why the supposed dream makes the scene on the street so unimportant, and I think the idea of 'some ultimate

---

[9] Lesley Chamberlain, *Nietzsche in Turin*. London: Quartet Books, 1996, p. 208.

[10] Ibid., p. 209. Trying to find an account of this dream, I came across something else, a little fable that Nietzsche says he thought up, and imagined discussing with Diderot. 'A winter landscape. An old coachman, who with the expression of the most brutal cynicism, harder than the winter around him, urinates on his own horse. The horse, the poor, flayed creature, looks around, thankful, *very* thankful.' Letter to Reinhart von Seydlitz, 13 May 1888. *Werke*, vol. III, p. 1294. My translation. Chamberlain appears to have lent Raskolnikov's dream to Nietzsche, but the philosopher's waking fable does also lead him to an actual horse on the Turin street. Cf Janz, *Friedrich Nietzsche: Biographie*, pp. 34–35.

autobiographical urge' will bear a little examination. But the echo of Dostoevsky is significant, and a nice instance of what I've been saying about the fictionable world.[11] It's always hard to know how much fictioning has already taken place.

III

In *The Unbearable Lightness of Being*, Kundera contemplates his character Tereza, and her sadness about no longer being able to give all her cows names:

> There were too many of them. Not so long before, forty years or so, all the cows in the village had names. (And if having a name is a sign of having a soul, I can say that they had souls despite Descartes.) But then the villages were turned into a large collective factory, and the cows began spending all their lives in the five square feet set aside for them in their cowsheds. From that time on, they have had no names and become mere *machinae animatae*. The world has proved Descartes correct.[12]

'Correct' here is of course deeply ironic, a mocking reconstruction of old Communist usage. Descartes is 'correct' in the sense that he understood modernity, and specifically the modernity of the socialist state, the collectivized farm, where the cows are just machines, no longer creatures with names. We note the swift, apparently casual thinking on the subject of souls, too. A name is the sign of having a soul, so if you don't have a name you don't have a

---

[11] The same unfortunate horse, or a close relative, appears in *The Secret Agent*, and is the object of the boy Stevie's distressed compassion. Of course, Nietzsche couldn't have read Conrad in 1907; but Conrad certainly read Dostoevsky, and probably knew the Nietzsche story.

[12] Milan Kundera, *The Unbearable Lightness of Being*. Translated by Michael Henry Heim. New York: Harper & Row, 1984, p. 290.

soul. Or rather, you do, as you always did, but no one talks
as if you have, and no one treats you as if you have. Kundera
is asking in what sense cows (or anyone) can have a soul if
there is no means of recognizing its presence.

Kundera says that he keeps seeing Tereza as she broods
on these sorry developments. And then he writes:

Another image also comes to mind: Nietzsche leaving his hotel in
Turin. Seeing a horse and a coachman beating it with a whip,
Nietzsche went up to the horse and, before the coachman's very
eyes, put his arms around the horse's neck and burst into tears.

That took place in 1889, when Nietzsche, too, had removed himself
from the world of people. In other words, it was at the time when his
mental illness had just erupted. But for that very reason I feel his
gesture has broad implications: Nietzsche was trying to apologize to
the horse for Descartes. His lunacy (that is, his final break with
mankind) began at the very moment he burst into tears over the
horse.[13]

The image of Nietzsche 'comes to mind'. The image of a
philosopher, the implication is, who thought that not only
Descartes but the whole march of modernity was wrong, and
wrong specifically about the relation of humankind to animals,
or about the kind of animals we are, and the kind of animals
animals are. Of course he was crazy, and his gesture occurs at
the moment of his craziness, but that is a sign of our plight, not
some accidental disaster of Nietzsche's mind. Lunacy is a 'break
with mankind', but so is a care for individual animals, and the
refusal of progress. The whole passage is oddly abstract, given
its content, but also mischievous. It pays no attention to
Nietzsche's actual madness, or indeed Nietzsche's actual views
at all. Nietzsche is not so much a philosopher here as philosophy

[13]   Ibid., p. 290.

itself, and the writing shows no interest in the possibility that Nietzsche's lunacy could be anything other than a rational refusal of what Kundera doesn't like. A curious equation is also being made between 'people' and the wrong kind of sanity. 'Nietzsche ... had removed himself from the world of people. In other words, it was at the time when his mental illness had just erupted.' 'People' think you have to be mad to refuse modernity and progress. Kundera wants to say that you only have to be properly unworldly, although in extreme cases it might take madness to land you in that condition.

Nietzsche and the horse make a startling and very moving appearance in Roland Barthes's essay on photography, *La Chambre claire*. Barthes is wondering whether one can fall in love with certain photographs, the way he suddenly fell in love, he says, with the figure of a female android in a film by Federico Fellini.

I then realized that there was a sort of link (or knot) between photography, madness and something whose name I did not know. I began by calling it: the pangs of love ['*la souffrance de l'amour*']. Was I not, in fact, in love with the Fellini automaton? Is one not in love with certain photographs? ... Yet it was not quite that ... In the love stirred by photography (by certain photographs), another music is heard, its name oddly old-fashioned: Pity ['*une autre musique se faisait entendre, au nom bizarrement démodé: la Pitié*']. I collected in a last thought the images which had 'pricked' me ... In each of them, inescapably, I passed beyond the unreality of the thing represented, I entered crazily into the spectacle, into the image, taking into my arms what is dead, what is going to die, as Nietzsche did, when on January 3, 1889, he threw himself in tears on the neck of a beaten horse: gone mad for Pity's sake ['*devenu fou pour cause de Pitié*'].[14]

---

[14] Roland Barthes, *La Chambre claire*. Paris: Gallimard Seuil, 1980, pp. 178–179. *Camera Lucida*. Translated by Richard Howard. New York: Hill and Wang, 1981, pp. 116–117.

Barthes is following Podach, whom he cites, but of course he is telling a quite different story. This is not a Nietzsche who feels pity and then goes mad. This is a Nietzsche whom pity drives to madness. It's mad to fall in love with a photograph, Barthes is saying, or with a figure in a film, but we have to name our feelings as we can, and love and pity are as close as he can get. An insane, an impossible pity accompanies an insane, impossible love. Pity is the right name for what we feel, Barthes finally thinks, but the object is wrong. We are feeling pity for a creature we cannot possibly reach through such feelings, or indeed through any feelings of ours. So we can read Barthes as saying slightly more than he literally says about Nietzsche.

Nietzsche goes mad through pity, but the pity itself is mad. He goes mad because he feels both the pity and the impossibility of it. His embrace of the horse is a sign of the impossibility and an attempt to transcend it. This is why it's important that it's an embrace, a human appeal, and not a gesture a horse could recognize, like stroking or the offer of food.

There is one more suggestion in Barthes's text. In feeling pity for an image, moving or not, we are feeling pity for the creature who has become that image, who is dead or going to die, in Barthes's phrase. All photographs say this to us, Barthes claims. 'That is dead and that is going to die.'[15] So most immediately of all, in this story, Nietzsche embraces the sheer mortality of the horse, embraces it because it is mortal. Its present suffering is a marker and prophecy of that fact, a sort of photograph of the horse's killable condition, and Nietzsche goes mad not for pity's sake but for mortality's

---

[15] *La Chambre claire*, p. 150; *Camera Lucida*, p. 96.

sake. Or he goes mad because of their conjunction, out of pity for sheer mortality.

IV

Nietzsche succumbs to pity; enacts a dream; apologizes for Descartes; goes mad because pity is both inevitable and impossible. He sobs, but does he laugh at any point? Where is the *gai saber*, *la gaya scienza*? This is what Bataille tries to show us. Or rather tries to show to a group of none too persuaded Catholic philosophers and others.

The occasion is a meeting held in Paris on 5 March 1944, and among those present, apart from the senior Catholic intellectuals, are Maurice Blanchot, Simone de Beauvoir, Albert Camus, Pierre Klossowski, Michel Leiris, Maurice Merleau-Ponty, Jean Paulhan, Jean Prévost and Jean-Paul Sartre. The people who, apart from Bataille, are the key players in the story as I see it speak up at the end. They are Jean Hyppolite and Gabriel Marcel, a Hegelian and a Catholic existentialist.

Bataille has given a paper called 'Le Rire de Nietzsche', 'Nietzsche's Laughter', and has argued that Nietzsche 'said no to life as long as it was easy; but yes when it took on the form of the impossible'. He quotes a late Nietzsche fragment: 'To see the shipwreck of tragic figures and to be able to laugh, in spite of the profound understanding, emotion and sympathy one feels, that is divine.' Bataille says that as humans we can laugh if we don't care about those who are shipwrecked or if it turns out they are not really shipwrecked at all, but then makes a curious, and characteristic switch, and puts himself into the wreck rather than in the position of the spectator. 'Laughing because I know I am going under, I am a god,' Bataille says. ('*Riant de me savoir sombrer, je suis*

un dieu.') 'Zarathustra made laughter *sacred*.'[16] The notion of
shipwreck dominates the whole of the ensuing discussion,
which gets very animated, precisely because Bataille has
claimed the right to laugh – if he wants to, and if the
shipwreck is his own. This has nothing much to do with
Nietzsche, and everything to with Bataille's Nietzscheanism.
But the scene in Turin is going to return.

A. M. de Gandillac asks if there is not 'a certain contradiction' between the lightness of spirit that Bataille has
invoked, 'this kind of joy and indifference', and 'the tragedy
of the situation in which you are deliberately enclosing
yourself'. De Gandillac sees Bataille as an unrepentant athe-
ist, and therefore not as a person who is entitled to laugh at
his own shipwreck, merely as a person who doesn't know
what a shipwreck is. Bataille staunchly says that he doesn't
see any contradiction. De Gandillac says, 'You do not
inhabit your contradiction permanently', which seems pretty
astute. Bataille answers, 'Nietzsche says we must perceive
the tragic and be able to laugh about it' – a rather violent
paraphrase of what he himself has said Nietzsche said, but he
is getting a little rattled, and he is on enemy ground.[17]
Nietzsche said it was divine to perceive the tragic and
laugh about it, and nothing about the availability of such
divinity to humans.

Bataille says that he has been speaking of laughter, but has
been represented as laughing sourly, literally laughing yellow, '*riant jaune*'. Yellow laughter, he says, is what is most
alien to him. And here's how the whole thing ends. A fine
piece of theatre.

---

[16] Georges Bataille, *Oeuvres complètes*. Paris: Gallimard, 1973, 12 vols., vol.
VI, p. 311. My translation.
[17] Ibid., p. 356.

Bataille:	I feel I am among you as the opposite of the person who calmly watches from the shore the ships which have lost their masts. I am on the ship which has lost its mast ... I am having a good time, and I laugh as I look at the people on the shore, I think, much more than anyone could laugh from the shore while looking at the mastless ship, because after all, I don't see that anyone could be so cruel as to laugh freely from the shore at a ship without a mast. If you're sinking, it's different, you can welcome it with a joyous heart [*s'en donner à coeur joie*].
Hyppolite:	It's Zarathustra's laughter.
Bataille:	If you like. In any case I'm amazed that people see it as so bitter.
Hyppolite:	Not bitter.
Marcel:	All the same, that story ended badly ... Just a historical point. [*C'est tout de même une histoire qui a mal finie ... Simple référence historique.*]
Bataille:	And?
Marcel:	Was Nietzsche still laughing in Turin? I'm not sure he was.
Bataille:	On the contrary, I believe he was laughing then.
De Gandillac:	We are not speaking about the laughter in Turin.
Bataille:	What does anything mean at that moment?[18]

For a long time I thought Bataille had simply lost this argument, found himself stranded in an untenable position, and in one sense he has. The gay science exists but it has its limits, and madness is one of them. Nietzsche was not laughing in Turin but sobbing, and this is not an Empsonian sobbing

---

[18] Ibid., pp. 358–359.

that includes its opposite. There is something heartless in
Bataille's insistence on the laughter, and something rather too
conventionally literary and unfelt, perhaps, in his idea of shipwreck. And there is genuine human compassion in Marcel's
unwillingness to believe that Nietzsche was laughing in Turin.
But there is also something sly and donnish about Marcel's
undercutting of Bataille, the appeal to the facts, the '*simple
référence historique*', and both Marcel and Bataille have managed, because they are arguing and busy solidifying their posi-
tions, to forget what Nietzsche was actually saying. Nietzsche's
idea requires not that he or any human should be laughing at
the scene in Turin, only that the gods could be. Laughing
without any diminution of their understanding and sympathy.

I'm afraid all the gods I have read about, and indeed all the
gods I can imagine laugh rather cruelly when they laugh at
all. But then is it impossible to imagine Nietzsche's implied
gods? Couldn't they be our instructors in a really new gay
science, the one meant, you will remember, as Bernard
Williams said, to defy the spirit of gravity? Some kinds of
laughter are perfectly compatible with understanding and
sympathy, indeed are forms of understanding and sympathy,
but that is not the same as laughing in a world of shipwreck.
Yet this is what Nietzsche was talking about, and it was
certainly the great lesson that Yeats took from Nietzsche,
whom he called, in a letter to Lady Gregory, 'that strong
enchanter'.[19] The lesson, learnable or not, is particularly
clear in the poem I quoted in my last chapter, 'Lapis Lazuli'.

> All perform their tragic play,
> There struts Hamlet, there is Lear,

[19] Cited in Keith M. May, *Nietzsche and Modern Literature*. Basingstoke:
Macmillan, 1988, p. 18

That's Ophelia, that Cordelia;
Yet they, should the last scene be there,
The great stage curtain about to drop,
If worthy their prominent part in the play,
Do not break up their lines to weep.
They know that Hamlet and Lear are gay;
Gaiety transfiguring all that dread ...

All things fall and are built again
And those that build them again are gay.

Two Chinamen, behind them a third,
Are carved in Lapis Lazuli ...

On all the tragic scene they stare.
One asks for mournful melodies;
Accomplished fingers begin to play.
Their eyes, mid many wrinkles, their eyes,
Their ancient, glittering eyes, are gay.[20]

Lear and Cordelia are gay, the builders are gay, but the ancient Chinamen are not characters in a play or builders, they are scarcely even spectators. They do know about ruin, though, and their eyes are gay from sheer knowledge. Can we intuit this knowledge, and will a poem or a story help us? Perhaps we can, and perhaps it will, but only after we have travelled a very considerable distance into the fictionable world. Meanwhile, Yeats is certainly persuasive about his longing for Nietzschean wisdom, and more convincing than Bataille on the possibility of a gaiety that would transfigure dread. '"Bitter and gay", that is the heroic mood', Yeats wrote in a letter to Dorothy Wellesley.[21] But longing, possibility and mood are still some way from the actual

[20] W. B. Yeats, *Collected Poems*. Edited by Richard J. Finneran. Basingstoke: Macmillan, 1989, pp. 294–295.
[21] Cited in May, *Nietzsche and Modern Literature*, p. 57.

achievement of divine laughter – of the laughter that would not after all be heartless.

V

Henry James, in 'The Future of the Novel', says that there is a challenge which fiction has 'never philosophically met'. It has never, to put it bluntly, done anything more philosophical about the challenge than just produce another novel, 'never defended its position by any better argument than the frank, straight blow: "Why am I not so unprofitable as to be preposterous? Because I can do *that*. There!" And it throws up from time to time some purely practical masterpiece.'[22] If James had read Borges or Calvino, or for that matter Wallace Stevens, he might have felt the challenge had at least been taken up. But he might also have felt that the particular challenge he had in mind was still lying in wait, would always be lying in wait, for fiction. He is interested in fiction's role as

mere unsupported and unguaranteed history, the *inexpensive* thing, written in the air, the record of what, in any particular case, has *not* been, the account that remains responsible, at best, to 'documents' with which we are practically unable to collate it. This is the side of the whole business of fiction on which it can be challenged, and to that degree that if the general venture had not become in such a manner the admiration of the world it might but too easily have become the derision.[23]

---

[22] Henry James, *Selected Literary Criticism*. Edited by Morris Shapira. Cambridge: Cambridge University Press, 1981, pp. 181–182.

[23] Ibid., p. 181.

The lordly swoop of the last sentence is funny in the best manner of the later James. He goes on to say that there is 'an admirable minority of intelligent persons' who can't see the point of reading novels, and another group who love novels but have stopped reading them because they have been disappointed by their recent reading experiences. 'The indifferent and the alienated', James says, 'testify ... almost as much as the omnivorous, to the reign of the great ambiguity, the enjoyment of which rests, evidently, on a primary need of the mind.'[24] There is a little shuffling of the deck here. The enjoyment of this particular type of ambiguity can't be a primary need of the mind if some people don't bother with it and others have given it up. James seems to be smuggling in an answer while pretending still be to asking the question, or he is just going a little too fast.

Now I am not going to rush in where Henry feared to tread – or rather both feared to tread and trod rather broadly after all – and I'm not going to try to meet his philosophical challenge. I do want to ask – and this is where I hope the idea of the fictionable world will help us – what it means that we can so regularly and so comfortably avoid the challenge, and indeed forget about it altogether for long stretches of time. We are not the indifferent or the alienated in matters of the novel, or literature more generally. We wouldn't even be considering this question if we were. But I think we harbour within us, and perhaps should harbour within us, modest relatives or representatives of those groups, inner subjects who do ask, now and again, why we should bother with a novel or a poem when there are other things to do, and why we shouldn't, after a long run of infinitely disappointing poems or novels, old or new, just give up the whole literary

---

[24] Ibid., p. 182.

project, and devote our time to Florentine painting or the late works of Ravel or Charlie Parker.

Two recent examples, or provocations, one pointing each way. That is, one towards asking why we bother to read novels, and one reminding us why we do. In the first case the critical gesture is so common that it would be invidious to pick out a particular reviewer. The gesture goes like this. A novelist has depicted, in a minor role, a member of one of society's hard-working classes, say a policeman or a nurse or a person employed at the supermarket checkout point — groups that perhaps neither the novelist nor the reviewer has any very intimate acquaintance of. The reviewer confidently says: This is exactly how policemen (or nurses or people working in supermarkets) talk (or think or behave), and praises the novelist for his or her exactitude. We can read this sort of claim every day, but just what is the claim? That this is how your typical policeman talks? Even if he's a policewoman? That this is how many, or most policeman talk? That this is how one policeman once talked? Well, let's raise the stakes. Suppose we settle these questions and decide the reviewer is right. This really is how a very substantial section of the police force talks, the social representation is as good as it can get. Why would this matter in a novel, and why would we go to a novel for this kind of information, when there are so many other, better places to go?

The answer to the second question is we don't — go to the novel for this kind of information. We used to, when we lived in the eighteenth and nineteenth centuries, and before the invention of photography, cinema and sociology, but we don't now. The long answer to the first question — why it may matter whether one gets such a thing right in a novel — is spread about this book, and has to do with what we might call the domestic and foreign affairs of literature, the relation

of a work to its own components and to the world outside it.
In Joyce's *Ulysses*, for example, it matters a lot that the right
historical ship docks in Dublin harbour on the right day, and
that the right historical horse wins the Gold Cup. The
novel's realism is part of its manners. But you are not
going to find Proust's Combray in the little town of Illiers,
even if it has changed its name to Illiers-Combray. Proust
doesn't log or clock the world as Joyce does. Even the
Dreyfus Affair appears in his novel only as refracted through
many minds. The short answer to the question is that what
we believe a novel shows us is always going to be more
important than the facts as we may get them from another
source. And in this sense our reviewer is telling us something
significant. Not about policemen but about reading. He or
she is telling us that the policeman is real enough for the
reader, and real enough for what appear to be the novel's
needs. But the reviewer isn't telling us why we should bother
to read novels. Rather the reverse – giving us reasons that
can't help us.

Reviewing John Banville's novel *Shroud*, Jack Miles
remarked that the novelist's language is 'a wonder', and for
that reason 'cannot fail to draw attention to itself'. The word
'trepidant', for example 'An out-of-the-way word. *The
Amercian Heritage Dictionary* does not list it. But you know
what it means, don't you, and can you think of an alternative
that would produce the same effect?'[25] The full clause is 'like
a trepidant swimmer approaching the dreaded water's
edge'.[26] On the cover of the English edition of *Shroud* we
can read Martin Amis saying something similar: 'The deval-
ued phrase "beautifully written" becomes hard currency in

[25] Jack Miles, 'The art of self-destruction', *Los Angles Times*, 8 June, 2003.
[26] John Banville, *Shroud*. London: Picador, 2002, p. 190.

the fiction of John Banville. He is a master, and his prose gives continuous sensual delight.' I fully share the enthusiasm being expressed here, but there is something slightly displaced in the form of its expression. It's as if we were to say that Nabokov writes beautifully in *Lolita* when what we mean is that he beautifully catches the way Humbert Humbert overwrites. 'Trepidant' is not exactly John Banville's word, a word he made up just for the pleasure of lilting sound and latinate effect.[27] It is part of the linguistic world of his character, a Belgian scholar whose English is a little suspect only because it is better than ours.

Most of Banville's novels take the form of skilled impersonation, recently of characters closely resembling historical figures, Anthony Blunt in *The Untouchable*, and Paul de Man, in *Shroud*. Well, Paul de Man and a touch of Louis Althusser, as Banville's note to the novel says. I don't know whether de Man ever used the word trepidant, but he certainly could have, and Banville's invention seems to me inspired, even uncanny, in the way it finds the right wrong word for the lexical universe of a native speaker of French who is a literary critic and theorist, and fancies himself, like Humbert Humbert, as a stylist. 'You can always count on a murderer', you will remember Humbert said, 'for a fancy

---

[27] Other words that Banville's Alex Vander likes are 'abradant', 'crepitant', 'tenebrous', 'pavonian'. *Shroud*, pp. 233, 259, 263, 265. 'Pavonian' appears to be a combination of 'pavonine' and 'favonian', both of which he could have found in *Lolita*. 'Trepidant', it turns out, is in the dictionary after all, or at least in the *Oxford English Dictionary* and *Chambers*. Robert Newsom reminded me of this, and provided me with wonderful examples of the word's older and more recent use: in a 1907 poem by Francis Thompson, and a 1997 sarcasm in the *Los Angeles Times*, addressing 'trepidant Republicans and Democrats alike'. Odd company for a character based on Paul de Man to be keeping, but perhaps a taste for latinate English is more widespread than I thought.

prose style.'[28] Even riskier than this, but also funnier, is Banville's ventriloquizing of what an Anthony Blunt figure might have thought when quizzed by the press about his conscience, about the possibility that his activities in espionage on behalf of Russia could have sent a number of British agents to their death.

> I kept my nerve in face of that pack of jackals from newspapers today. *Did men die because of you?* Yes, dearie, swooned quite away. But no, no, I was superb, if I do say so myself. Cool, dry, balanced, every inch the Stoic: Coriolanus to the general. I am a great actor, that is the secret of my success.

The character goes on to quote Nietzsche: 'Must not anyone who wants to move the crowd be an actor who impersonates himself?'[29]

Such cases – and literature is full of such cases – raise our question about literature and knowledge in its most extreme form. Here are styles and reactions which we know are made up, which we can almost see being made up. How can there be knowledge here, if we know the writer is not even guessing, but plainly fabricating? This is not the plausible, generic policeman, but a particular instance of the frankly fictive, of what happens when a piece of historical life is seized upon as fictionable. This is, as James said, 'mere unsupported and unguaranteed history, the *inexpensive* thing, written in the air, the record of what, in any particular case, has *not* been . . . ' I don't think it's inexpensive in terms of labour, but James presumably means that fiction doesn't incur real-life costs. I'm not sure about that either. And

---

[28] Vladimir Nabokov, *Lolita*. London: Penguin, 1980, p. 1
[29] John Banville, *The Untouchable*. New York: Vintage, 1998, p. 9.

again, as I keep saying throughout this book, I don't know for sure that knowledge is what we are getting here. But when the man who calls himself Axel Vander thinks and speaks in *Shroud*, when Victor Maskell speaks and writes in *The Untouchable*, we are learning not what Paul de Man and Anthony Blunt might have thought and spoken and written – this could have been anything, the field is unlimited – but what their precisely realized shadows did think and speak and write, word for word. This can't count, except obliquely, as knowledge of de Man and Blunt – although you wouldn't expect me to say that oblique knowledge wasn't a good thing. But then what does it count as directly? In plain language, there is no mystery here. These are novels, and novels of a particular kind. They tell the fictional lives of historical people, just as many – perhaps most – novels tell the fictional lives of their own fictional people, the locals, so to speak, and others tell the fictional lives of people borrowed from other novels. There are good and bad novels about historical people, as there are of any other kind, and I don't want to make any special claim for novels of this sort. Or rather only a claim about the degree of intensity they lend to James's philosophical challenge. I want to say that when they are well done, they bring the question of literature and knowledge to the peculiar crunch I am trying to identify. These novels, I suggest, show us not the fictional lives of real people but the real lives of people who came extraordinarily close to existing, and I'm going to try to make that cryptic claim clearer by looking a little more closely at *Shroud*.

VI

Paul de Man, a distinguished literary critic and scholar, Professor of Comparative Literature at Cornell and Yale

and other places, wrote a series of articles for a collaborationist newspaper in Belgium during the Second World
War, two of them notably, and later notoriously, anti-
Semitic. The articles were rediscovered after de Man's
death, and caused quite a stir, particularly among his friends
and admirers, but also among his enemies, people who had
a distaste for deconstruction, which in the United States
at least was largely associated with de Man's name. He
had brought Derrida to the United States – in both senses.
He had invited Derrida to teach at Yale, and he had spread
the word about Derrida's work. De Man's version of deconstruction, for reasons that may seem more obvious than they
are, was quite a bit less political than Derrida's. I remembered being troubled, long before any revelations were
made, by the weird moral music in certain sentences of
Allegories of Reading. 'There can never be enough guilt
around to match the text-machine's infinite power to excuse';
'it is always possible to face up to any experience (to excuse
any guilt), because the experience always exists simultaneously as fictional discourse and as empirical event'.[30]
What I heard in these cadences was their ostensible meaning,
of course, but also something like its opposite, some sort of
lurking horror, and I wondered what the man had done.
Excuses are always possible, he seemed to be saying, but
where shall we find forgiveness?

Banville's character, like de Man, is interested in
Nietzsche, Rilke, Rousseau and the English Romantics, and
has written a series of oblique, ironic critical works on these
and other figures and topics. I don't think you need to know
about de Man's life and posthumous disgrace to read the
novel; you need only to know that someone like de Man

[30] De Man, *Allegories of Reading*, pp. 299, 293.

could have existed – in this case, as Aristotle would say,
could have because he did. And indeed it may well be that
the novel could lead one to de Man's life rather than the other
way round. But it's also useful to see what, in Banville's
hands, becomes fictionable about de Man's career. A great
deal, in one sense. Almost nothing, in another.

There is Belgium, the war years, the collaborationist articles, the hidden disgrace, the critical interests and writings
I have just mentioned, the long years in the United States,
increasing fame, the international lecture circuit. But then
think of all the things de Man didn't do, or have happen to
him, that are so firmly attached to his shadow in *Shroud*. He
didn't kill his ageing, Alzheimer's-afflicted wife; he wasn't
found out in his lifetime, and he didn't go to Turin to meet his
accuser. He didn't have an affair with her, a young woman
called Catherine Cleave, a refugee from another Banville
novel. He didn't *not* write the collaborationist articles, or
assume the identity of the person who had. But I don't want
to give any more of the plot away. You see we are deep into
'the record of what . . . has *not* been', as James puts it. We can
ask our question about knowledge again.

But first I need to say a little more about the language of
Banville's novel. I compared its narrative situation to that of
Nabokov's *Lolita*, where apart from the parodic Foreword,
the whole text is offered to us as Humbert Humbert's, as a
memoir he has drafted in prison after his murder of Clare
Quilty. I think this is ultimately the situation in *Shroud*, too:
that is, we must see the whole text as the creation of the man
who calls himself Axel Vander, but it's not immediately
obvious that this is the case, and since the phrase about the
trepidant swimmer appears in a piece of third-person narrative, and indeed a sentence that describes Vander from the
outside, it's not unreasonable for the American reviewer to

attribute this language to Banville himself. Not unreasonable, but not quite right, and the clues mount up precisely around this passage.

A page or so later, we read, 'Vander was watching her, turning his head on the pillow to follow her about the room with his eyes. He bade her eat. She brought a chair and sat down before the food. She was not hungry now. She was thinking. She was excited.' Who says she was thinking? Who says she was excited? The novelist. The impersonal narrator who has been taking turns with Vander himself so far. Wait a minute. Vander holds up his hand and says, 'With this I wrote those articles that you found. Not a single cell survives in it from that time. Then whose hand is it?' And without warning the prose moves into the first person, and into Vander's memory of his killing of his wife.

He, I, I saw again the empty bottle on its side, the mauve pills in my palm. I closed my eyes. I listened to the wind washing over the rooftops. The girl rose and came forward and knelt beside the bed and took my hand in both of hers and brought it to her lips and kissed it. I.[31]

And we remember that the book began with the words 'Who speaks?', and that on the third page Vander promised to explain himself to the now-dead girl. Well, we didn't know at that stage that she would be dead.

But the point here is not to establish the work's narrative point of view, essential as such precautions are. The point is to suggest that the novel has, in its most intimate verbal details, the colour of Vander's mind, to borrow an image from Emily Brontë Syntax, vocabulary, imagery, rhythms,

[31] Banville, *Shroud*, pp. 192–193.

silences – everything about the language is a picture of this man. Promising to explain himself, Vander also promised to talk calmly and quietly, and to eschew his 'accustomed gaudiness of tone and gesture'. Fortunately, he hasn't done anything of the kind. It's hard to think that 'concumbance' and 'brumously' are Catherine Cleave's words, although they appear in accounts of her thoughts. Here is Vander in Turin:

They all know me by now, the baker and the butcher and the fellow at the vegetable stall, and their customers too, hennaed housewives, mostly, plump as pigeons, with their perfume and jewellery and great, dark, disappointed eyes ... Clearly I interest them. Perhaps what appeals to them is the suggestion of commedia dell'arte in my appearance, the one-eyed glare and comically spavined gait, the stick and hat in place of Harlequin's club and mask ...

Turin resembles nothing so much as a vast, grandiose cemetery, with all this marble, these monuments, these gesturing statues; it is no wonder poor N. went off his head here, thinking himself a king and the father of kings and stopping in the street to embrace a cabman's nag. They lost his luggage, too, as once they did mine, sent it to Sampierdarena when he was headed in the opposite direction ...

And here is Vander on his American disguise:

I dislike the smoke-and-ashes taste of bourbon, but early on I had fixed on it to be my drink, as part of my strategy of difference, another way of being on guard, as an actor puts a pebble in his shoe to remind him that the character he is playing has a limp. This was in the days when I was making myself over. So difficult it was, to judge just so, to forge the fine distinctions, to maintain a balance – no one would know how difficult. If it had been a work of art I was fashioning they would have applauded my mastery. Perhaps that was my mistake, to do it all secretly, instead of openly, with a flourish. They would have been entertained; they would have forgiven me; Harlequin is always forgiven, always survives.[32]

---

[32] Ibid., pp. 5, 3–4, 9–10.

But Vander is not Harlequin, only looks like him, and he doesn't want to be forgiven, only to survive. Nothing could be finer, more intimate with his ugly wit and truculence than the ambiguity of the phrase 'forge the fine distinctions'. To forge as on an anvil, and to forge as one fakes a banknote. But everything here is intimate with Vander's nasty psyche. We know the colour of his mind. Whose mind is this, and what does it mean to know it? It is not de Man's mind, and not Banville's mind. But it is someone's. It is a mind that only accidentally, we might say, failed to exist, if it has failed to exist. Such an argument would bring us close to Fielding's sly defence of fiction in *Joseph Andrews*. Historians get the dates and places right but the people wrong, he said. Novelists and playwrights get the people right but mysteriously put them in the wrong times and places. It was clearly a mistake for Cervantes to set *Don Quixote* in Spain, since one could see its characters in London any day.[33] I'm suggesting that even without the transferred incarnations we can't be sure that imaginary people are not real. 'Who can boast', to return to the Borges question I was commenting on in an earlier chapter, 'of being a mere imposter?'

Shroud has an epigraph from Nietzsche. 'We set up a word at the point at which our ignorance begins, at which we can see no further, e.g., the word "I", the word "do", the word "suffer": — these are perhaps the horizon of our knowledge, but not "truths".'[34] I do suffer. Here Nietzsche is not apologizing for

---

[33] Henry Fielding, *Joseph Andrews*. New York: Signet, 1961, p. 160. 'The facts we deliver may be relied on, though we often mistake the age and country wherein they happened: for though it may be worth the examination of critics whether the shepherd Chrysostom, who, as Cervantes informs us, died for love of the fair Marcella, who hated him, was ever in Spain, will any one doubt but that such a silly fellow hath really existed?'

[34] Nietzsche, *The Will to Power*, p. 267.

Descartes but parodying him. *Je souffre, donc je suis*. And of
course the novel is set in Turin because of Nietzsche –
Nietzsche has lured both Vander and Banville there. Vander
has not only written about Nietzsche's collapse in his book *After
Words* – 'a chapter . . . justly famous, if I may say so, on poor
Nietzsche's last, calamitous days here in Turin' – he reads this
famous chapter at an academic conference in Turin. He does
this because he hasn't bothered to prepare a paper, and because
he thinks it's a fine form of insult, even cruelty, to make the
conference participants listen to a work he knows they have all
read. Read and disliked, a number of them, since Vander says
that his book offers an 'admittedly skittish treatment of
[Nietzsche's] final transfiguration and collapse on the Piazza
Carlo Alberto'. Having had a lot to drink at lunch ('a bottle of
red wine . . . and . . . repeated jolts of grappa'), Vander takes
the girl who has found him out to visit the house where
Nietzsche lodged. 'Come with me,' he says, 'I want to show
you a place where an old friend of mine used to live.' 'You
see', he says, pointing to the name Fino on the door – the
name we have already met in Podach's account, the name of
Nietzsche's landlord. A young woman opens the door:

She held her hands joined before her, moving them about each other in a
slow, caressing, washing motion. I asked if we might be allowed inside to
see the room where the philosopher had lived. She frowned, and her
hands stopped moving. 'Nietzsche,' I said, loudly. 'Friedrich Nietzsche!'
The name sounded absurd, like a sneeze; it was swallowed in the
stairwell and rang back an echo that seemed to snigger. The young
woman pondered . . . She shook her head slowly. No one of that name
lived here, she said.. 'I don't mean *now*,' I said, fairly bellowing. 'A long
time ago! He lived here. *Il grande filosofo!*' I pointed again to the name on
the door, I mentioned the plaque on the wall outside. She would only
keep on shaking her head, remote, unapologetic, immovable.[35]

[35] Bounville, *Shroud*, pp. 150, 152, 99, 104, 108–109.

Il grande filosofo. The gods do seem to be laughing here, but one would rather they were weeping. Axel Vander is the sort of fellow who gives the gay science a bad name. But the novel he is in, the whole stylistic performance, does surely offer us at least the chance of knowledge, an instance, to borrow Bernard Williams's phrasing again, of 'hard and rigorous thought ... meant to convey a certain spirit, one that ... could defy the "spirit of gravity"'. Gravity here might mean literalness, or an unwillingness to spend time with imaginary real people. Somewhere between what Nietzsche calls the horizon of our knowledge and what he calls truths is the whole realm of what writers and readers and texts make of the fictionable world.

Epilogue: The essays of our life

There is a haunting passage in *The Man Without Qualities* where Musil gives us his precise and slightly melancholy definition of what he calls essayism. He has been arguing that there is something fantastic about the scientific attention to contemporary facts, and something pedantic about the humanistic attention to age-old fantasies: an intricate rehearsal of the Two Cultures debate. 'For what are we to do on the Last Day, when the works of humankind are weighed, with three treatises on formic acid, or even thirty? On the other hand, what do we know about the Last Day, if we don't even know what can be done with formic acid between now and then?' Musil's character Ulrich at first tries to negotiate these (and other) questions through the concept of 'hypothetical life': 'the present time is nothing but a hypothesis we have not yet got beyond'. Later he settles on the notion of the essay. 'Roughly as an essay ... takes a thing from many sides without grasping it whole ... he thought he could best see and respond to the world and his own life.' But isn't such a theory just an expression of insecurity? Musil allows for this possibility, but mischievously adds that 'insecurity is ... nothing but the insufficiency of the usual securities'.[1] An essayist manages

---

[1] Robert Musil, *Der Mann ohne Eigenschaften*. Hamburg: Rowohlt, 1970, pp. 248–251. *The Man Without Qualities*. Translated by Eithne Wilkins and

to stay close to the 'mobility of facts' – and also get beyond the treatise on formic acid.

An essay in this sense is not just an attempt at something, a bright idea or the sketch of a future truth. It contains its own meaning, but we are still at some distance from the completeness of Nietzsche's idea of the world as an aesthetic phenomenon or the stylishness of Wilde's suggestion of life as a work of art. 'An essay', Musil says, 'is the unique and unalterable form the inner life of a person takes in a decisive thought.' And the next, different thought is the next essay. Could one live in such a piecemeal way? Musil thinks so:

There have been not a few such essayists and masters of the floating inner life but no purpose would be served by naming them. Their domain lies between religion and knowledge, between example and doctrine, between *amor intellectualis* and poetry, they are saints with and without religion, and sometimes too they are simply men who have gone out on an adventure and lost their way. [2]

There is something very moving in the thought that an essayist may be just someone who got lost. And surely this is the risk and the reward of the adventure. We may discover the riches that lie in the spaces between disciplines and practices, for there must be riches there, and answers to many of our too sharply bifurcating questions. But we may discover only the spaces themselves and be left in the desert, peering into the walled cities where everyone else seems at home. Literature itself as I have been trying to portray it may assume the figure of the essayist, every poem and novel a decisive (but speculative) thought held in a unique and

Ernst Kaiser. London: Secker & Warburg, 1953, 2 vols., vol. I. pp. 294–298. Translation slightly modified.

[2] Ibid., pp. 253–254, 301.

unalterable form, every reading or rereading another moment among the essays of our life. And at this point I think I can bring together the two terms I have so carefully been keeping apart: literature and fiction. Literature is a body of works and fiction names a relation to reality. The terms overlap in much of what they include, but not all literature is fiction, and there are plenty of fictions outside literature. But literature is fiction in the fullest, most powerful sense when it sets out to encounter real knowledge along imaginary roads. The 'usual securities' are abandoned, and the roads cannot, outside of psychosis, lead directly back into the real. It's important to remember, too, that just getting lost on the journey is always possible. But there are many ways of meeting knowledge, and many knowledges to meet. Who can boast of being a mere imposter?

Bibliography

Aarsleff, Hans *From Locke to Saussure*. Minneapolis: University of Minnesota Press, 1982.

'Introduction', E. B. de Condillac, *Essay on the Origin of Human Knowledge*. Cambridge: Cambridge University Press, 2001.

Adorno, T. W. *Minima Moralia*. Frankfurt: Suhrkamp, 1951. Translated by Edmund Jephcott. London: Verso, 1978.

Aristotle *Poetics*. Translated by S. H. Butcher. New York: Hill and Wang, 1961.

Attridge, Derek *The Singularity of Literature*. London: Routledge, 2004.

Auden, W. H. *Collected Poems*. London: Faber & Faber, 1991.

Austin, J. L. *How To Do Things With Words*. Edited by J. O. Urmson. New York: Oxford University Press, 1965.

Sense and Sensibilia. Edited by G. J. Warnock. Oxford: Oxford University Press, 1964.

Banville, John *Eclipse*. New York: Vintage, 2002.

Shroud. London: Picador, 2002.

The Untouchable. New York: Vintage, 1998.

Barthes, Roland *La Chambre claire*. Paris: Gallimard Seuil, 1980. *Camera Lucida*. Translated by Richard Howard. New York: Hill and Wang, 1981.

Leçon. Paris: Seuil, 1978. Translated by Richard Howard in *A Barthes Reader*, ed. Susan Sontag. London: Jonathan Cape, 1982.

Sade, Fourier, Loyola. Paris: Seuil, 1971. Translated by Richard Miller. New York: Hill and Wang, 1976.

Bataille, Georges *Oeuvres complètes*. Paris: Gallimard, 1970–1990, 12 vols.

Benjamin, Walter *Illuminationen*. Frankfurt: Suhrkamp, 1977. *Illuminations*. Translated by Harry Zohn. New York: Schocken, 1969.

    One Way Street. Translated by Edmund Jephcott/Kingsley Shorter. London: Verso, 1979.

Bersani, Leo *The Culture of Redemption*. Cambridge: Harvard University Press, 1990.

    A Future for Astyanax. Boston: Little, Brown, 1976.

Bishop, Elizabeth *The Collected Prose*. New York: Farrar, Straus and Giroux, 1984.

    The Complete Poems. New York: Farrar, Straus and Giroux, 1979.

    One Art. New York: Farrar, Straus and Giroux, 1994.

Bohlman, Otto *Yeats and Nietzsche*. London: Macmillan, 1982.

Bolla, Peter de *Art Matters*. Cambridge: Harvard University Press, 2001.

Borges, Jorge Luis *Ficciones*. Buenos Aires: Emece, 1956. Translated by Anthony Kerrigan. New York: Grove Press, 1962.

Brod, Max *Franz Kafka: A Biography*. Translated by G. Humphreys Roberts and Richard Winston. New York: Da Capo Press, 1995.

Calvino, Italo *Le città invisibili*. Milan: Mondadori, 1993. *Invisible Cities*. Translated by William Weaver. New York: Harcourt Brace Jovanovich, 1974.

Cameron, Sharon *Thinking in Henry James*. Chicago: University of Chicago Press, 1989.

Carter, Miranda *Anthony Blunt: His Lives*. London: Pan, 2002.

Cavell, Stanley *The Claim of Reason*. Oxford: Clarendon Press, 1979.

    Disowning Knowledge in Six Plays of Shakespeare. Cambridge: Cambridge University Press, 1987.

    Must We Mean What We Say? Cambridge: Cambridge University Press, 1976.

Cervantes, Miguel de *Don Quixote*. Madrid: Austral, 1998. Translated by Edith Grossman. New York: HarperCollins, 2003.

Chamberlain, Lesley *Nietzsche in Turin*. London: Quartet Books, 1996.

Chatman, Seymour *The Later Style of Henry James*. Oxford: Blackwell, 1972.

Clark, Maudmarie *Nietzsche on Truth and Philosophy*. Cambridge: Cambridge University Press, 1990.

Coetzee, J. M. *Elizabeth Costello: Eight Lessons*. London: Secker & Warburg, 2003.

Collini, Stefan *English Pasts*. Oxford: Oxford University Press, 1999.

Condillac, E. B. de *Essai sur l'origine des connaissances humaines*. Paris: Editions Galilée, 1973.

Conrad, Joseph *Heart of Darkness*. New York: Norton, 1971.

Craig, Edward *Knowledge and the State of Nature*. Oxford: Clarendon Press, 1990.

Derrida, Jacques *De la grammatologie*. Paris: Editions de Minuit, 1967.

Donoghue, Denis 'Yeats: the New Political Issue', *Princeton University Library Chronicle*, vol. 59, no. 3, Spring 1998.

Dupee, F. W. 'Afterword', Henry James, *The Wings of the Dove*. New York: Signet, 1964.

Dupuy, J-P *Aux Origines des sciences cognitives*. Paris: La Découverte, 1999.

Eliot, T. S. *The Complete Poems and Plays*. New York: Harcourt, Brace & World, 1971.

Knowledge and Experience in the Philosophy of F. H. Bradley. New York: Farrar, Straus, 1964.

Empson, William *The Complete Poems*. Edited by John Haffenden. London: Penguin, 2001.

Seven Types of Ambiguity. New York: New Directions, 1966.

Some Versions of Pastoral. New York: New Directions, 1974.

Using Biography. London: Chatto & Windus, 1984.

Fielding, Henry *Joseph Andrews*. New York: Signet, 1961.

Fisher, Philip *The Vehement Passions*. Princeton: Princeton University Press, 2002.

Fodor, Jerry *In Critical Condition*. Cambridge: MIT Press, 1998.

Ford, Andrew *The Origins of Criticism*. Princeton: Princeton University Press, 2002.

Foucault, Michel *L'Archéologie du savoir*. Paris: Gallimard, 1969.

Les Mots et les choses. Paris: Gallimard, 1966.

Surveiller et punir: naissance de la prison. Paris: Gallimard, 1975.

Frankfurt, Harry G. *The Importance of What We Care About*. Cambridge: Cambridge University Press, 1988.

The Reasons of Love. Princeton: Princeton University Press, 2004.

Freedman, Jonathan *Professions of Taste*. Stanford: Stanford University Press, 1990.

Fry, Paul H. *A Defense of Poetry*. Stanford: Stanford University Press, 1995.

William Empson: Prophet Against Sacrifice. London: Routledge, 1991.

Garber, Marjorie *A Manifesto for Literary Studies*. Seattle: University of Washington, 2003.

Gardner, Philip and Averil *The God Approached*. Totoua, N. J.: Rowman and Littlefield, 1978.

Gill, Christopher, and T. P. Wiseman *Lies and Fiction in the Ancient World*. Exeter: University of Exeter Press, 1993.

Gossman, Lionel *Between History and Literature*. Cambridge: Harvard University Press, 1990.

Gourgouris, Stathis *Does Literature Think?* Stanford: Stanford University Press, 2003.

Graves, Robert *The Greek Myths*. Harmondsworth: Penguin, 1960, 2 vols.

Grice, Paul *Studies in the Way of Words*. Cambridge: Harvard University Press, 1989.

Guillory, John *Cultural Capital*. Chicago: University of Chicago Press, 1993.

'The Sokal Affair and the History of Criticism', *Critical Inquiry*, vol. 28, no. 2, Winter 2002.

Habermas, Jürgen *Knowledge and Human Interests*. Translated by Jeremy J. Shapiro. Boston: Beacon Press 1972.

The Philosophical Discourse of Modernity. Translated by Fredrick G. Lawrence. Cambridge: MIT Press, 1990.

Hagberg, G. L. *Art as Language*. Ithaca: Cornell University Press, 1995.

Harries, Martin *Scare Quotes from Shakespeare*. Stanford: Stanford University Press, 2000.

Heidegger, Martin *Unterwegs ʒur Sprache*. Pfullingen: Verlag Gunther Neske, 1959.

On the Way to Language. Translated by Peter D. Hertz. San Francisco: HarperCollins, 1982.

Heller, Joseph *Catch-22*. New York: Simon & Schuster, 2003.

Hesiod *Theogony*. Translated by Norman O. Brown. Indianapolis: Bobbs-Merrill, 1953.

Hill, Geoffrey *Collected Poems*. Harmondsworth: Penguin, 1985.

Hirschman, Albert O. *The Passions and the Interests*. Princeton: Princeton University Press, 1997.

Hungerford, Amy *The Holocaust of Texts*. Chicago: University of Chicago Press, 2003.

James, Henry *The Art of the Novel*. New York: Charles Scribner's Sons, 1962.

'The Beast in the Jungle', in *Complete Tales*. Edited by Leon Edel. London: Rupert Hart-Davis, 1964.

'The Jolly Corner', in *Selected Tales*. Edited by Peter Messent/ Tom Paulin. London: Everyman, 1983.

Selected Literary Criticism. Edited by Morris Shapira. Cambridge: Cambridge University Press, 1981.

What Maisie Knew. London: Penguin, 1966.

The Wings of the Dove. London: Penguin, 1986.

Janz, Curt Paul *Friedrich Nietzsche: Biographie*. Munich: Hanser, 1979.

Jaspers, Karl *Nietzsche*. Translated by Charles F. Wallraff and Frederick J. Schmitz. Baltimore: Johns Hopkins University Press, 1997.

Joyce, James *Portrait of the Artist as a Young Man*. New York: Viking, 1964.

Kafka, Franz 'Brief an den Vater', in *Hochzeitsvorbereitungen auf dem Lande*. Frankfurt: Fischer, 1991.

'The Metamorphosis', in *The Complete Stories*. Translated by Willa and Edwin Muir. New York: Schocken Books, 1971.

Der Proceß. Frankfurt: Fischer, 1993. *The Trial*. Translated by Breon Mitchell. New York: Schocken Books, 1998.

Sämtliche Erzählungen. Frankfurt: Fischer, 1970.

Metamorphosis and Other Stories. Translated by Malcolm Pasley. London: Penguin, 2000.

Kalstone, David *Becoming a Poet*. New York: Farrar, Straus and Giroux, 1989.

Kripke, Saul *Naming and Necessity*. Cambridge: Harvard University Press, 1980.

Wittgenstein on Rules and Private Language. Cambridge: Harvard University Press, 1982.

Krook, Dorothea *The Ordeal of Consciousness in Henry James*. Cambridge: Cambridge University Press, 1967.

Kundera, Milan *The Unbearable Lightness of Being*. Translated by Michael Henry Heim. New York: Harper & Row, 1984.

Leighton, Angela 'Elegies of Form in Bishop, Plath, Stevenson', *Proceedings of the British Academy* vol. 121, 2002.

Gallez, Paula Le *The Rhys Woman*. Basingstoke: Macmillan, 1990.

Levi, Primo *The Drowned and the Saved*. Translated by Raymond Rosenthal. New York: Vintage, 1989.

    If This is a Man, later published as *Survival in Auschwitz*. Translated by Stuart Woolf. New York: Simon & Schuster, 1996.

Levine, George *Dying to Know*. Chicago: University of Chicago Press, 2002.

Levi-Strauss, Claude *Tristes tropiques*. Paris: Plon, 1955.

Lewis, David K. *On the Plurality of Worlds*. Oxford: Blackwell, 1986.

Lingua Franca, ed. *The Sokal Hoax*. Lincoln: University of Nebraska Press, 2000.

Lodge, David *Consciousness and the Novel*. Cambridge: Harvard University Press, 2002.

    Thinks. New York: Penguin, 2001.

Lyotard, Jean-François *La condition postmoderne: rapport sur le savoir*. Paris: Editions de Minuit, 1979.

    Lectures d'enfance. Paris: Editions Galilée, 1991.

Macherey, Pierre *A quoi pense la littérature?* Paris: Presses universitaires de France, 1990.

MacLeish, Archibald *Collected Poems*. Boston: Houghton Mifflin, 1962.

Man, Paul de *Allegories of Reading*. New Haven: Yale University Press, 1979.

    Blindness and Insight. Oxford: Oxford University Press, 1971.

    The Resistance to Theory. Minneapolis: University of Minnesota Press, 1986.

Marlowe, Christopher *Doctor Faustus*. London: Methuen, 1965.

May, Keith M. *Nietzsche and Modern Literature*. Basingstoke: Macmillan, 1988.

McCabe, Susan *Elizabeth Bishop: Her Poetics of Loss*. University Park, Pa.: Pennsylvania State University Press, 1994.

McCormick, John *Fiction as Knowledge*. New Brunswick: Transaction, 1999.

McFarland, Ronald E. *The Villanelle: Evolution of a Poetic Form.* Moscow, Idaho: University of Idaho Press, 1987.

McGann, Jerome J. *Towards a Literature of Knowledge.* Chicago: University of Chicago Press, 1989.

McGinn, Colin *Knowledge and Reality.* Oxford: Clarendon Press, 1999.

Medawar, Peter *Pluto's Republic.* Oxford: Oxford University Press, 1982.

Millier, Brett C. *Elizabeth Bishop: Life and the Memory of It.* Berkeley: University of California Press, 1993.

Milton, John *Paradise Lost,* in *Poetical Works.* Oxford: Oxford University Press, 1969.

Monteiro, George *Conversations with Elizabeth Bishop.* Jackson: University Press of Mississippi, 1996.

Moran, Richard *Authority and Estrangement.* Princeton: Princeton University Press, 2001.

Muldoon, Paul *Poems 1968–1998.* London: Faber & Faber, 2001.

Musil, Robert *Der Mann ohne Eigenschaften.* Hamberg: Rowohlt, 1970. *The Man Without Qualities.* Translated by Eithne wilkins and Ernst Kaiser. London: Secker & Warburg, 1953, 2 vols, vol. I.

Nabokov, Vladimir *Ada.* London: Penguin, 1971.

Lolita. London: Penguin, 1980.

The Real Life of Sebastian Knight. Norfolk: New Directions, 1959.

Nehamas, Alexander *Nietzsche: Life as Literature.* Cambridge: Harvard University Press, 1985.

Nietzsche, Friedrich *The Gay Science.* Translated by Josefine Nauckhoff and Adrian del Caro. Cambridge: Cambridge University Press, 2001.

The Will to Power. Translated by Walter Kauffman and R. J. Hollingdale. New York: Vintage, 1968, p. 199.

Werke. Edited by Karl Schlechta. Munich: Hanser, 1966, 3 vols.

Nussbaum, Martha *The Fragility of Goodness.* Cambridge: Cambridge University Press, 2001.

Love's Knowledge. Oxford: Oxford University Press, 1992.

Poetic Justice. Boston: Beacon Press, 1995.

Ozick, Cynthia *What Henry James Knew.* London: Jonathan Cape, 1993.

Passerat, Jean *Les Poésies françaises.* Paris: A. Lemerre, 1880, 2 vols, vol. II.

Pfister, Manfred 'Die Villanelle in der englischen Moderne', *Archiv für das Studium der neueren Sprachen und Literaturen*, vol. 219, no. 2, 1982.

Pippin, Robert *Henry James and Modern Moral Life*. Cambridge: Cambridge University Press, 2000.

Plato *Republic*. Translated by C. M. A. Grube. Indianapolis: Hackett, 1992.

Podach, E. F. *Nietzsches Zusammenbruch*. Heidelberg: Kampmann Verlag, 1930.

Powers, Richard *Galatea 2.2*. New York: Farrar, Straus and Giroux, 1995.

Proust, Marcel *Contre Sainte-Beuve*. Paris: Gallimard, 1971.

   A la recherche du temps perdu. Paris: Gallimard, 1987–1989, 4 vols. *In Search of Lost Time*. Translated by Lydia Davis, James Grieve, Mark Treharne, John Sturrock, Carol Clark, Peter Collier, Ian Patterson. London: Penguin, 2002.

Rhys, Jean *Good Morning, Midnight*. London: Penguin, 1969.

Richards, I. A. *Principles of Literary Criticism*. New York: Harcourt, Brace & World, 1961.

   Poetries and Sciences. New York, Norton, 1970.

Ricks, Christopher *The Force of Poetry*. Oxford: Clarendon Press, 1984.

Righter, William *American Memory in Henry James*. Aldershot and Burlington: Ashgate, 2004.

   The Myth of Theory. Cambridge: Cambridge University Press, 1994.

Rilke, Rainer Maria *Ausgewählte Gedichte*. Frankfurt: Suhrkamp, 1966. *Selected Poetry*. Translated by Stephen Mitchell. New York: Vintage, 1989.

Rose, Gillian *Mourning Becomes the Law*. Cambridge: Cambridge University Press, 1996.

Rose, Jacqueline *Albertine*. London: Chatto & Windus, 2001.

Rushdie, Salman *Shame*. London: Picador, 1984.

Sartre, Jean-Paul *L'Imaginaire: psychologie phénoménologique de l'imagination*. Paris: Gallimard, 1978.

   Qu'est-ce que la littérature? Paris: Gallimard, 2002.

Schrift, Alan D. *Nietzsche's French Legacy*. London: Routledge, 1995.

Schwartz, Lloyd, and Sybil Estess, eds. *Elizabeth Bishop and Her Art*. Ann Arbor: University of Michigan Press, 1983.

Shakespeare, William *Macbeth*. Edited by A. R. Braunmüller. Cambridge: Cambridge University Press, 1997.

Shelley, P. B. 'A Defence of Poetry', in *Shelley's Poetry and Prose*, Edited by D. H. Reiman/Neil Fraistat. New York: Norton, 2002.

Sidney, Philip *A Defence of Poetry*. Edited by Jan van Dorsten. Oxford: Oxford University Press, 1966.

Simpson, David *The Academic Postmodern and the Rule of Literature*. Chicago: University of Chicago Press, 1995.

Spivak, Gayatri *Death of a Discipline*. New York: Columbia University Press, 2003.

Stern, J. P. *Hitler: The Führer and the People*. London: Fontana, 1984.
A Study of Nietzsche. Cambridge: Cambridge University Press, 1979.
'The World of Ravensbrück', *Cambridge Review*, 6 June 1964.
and M. S. Silk *Nietzsche on Tragedy*. Cambridge: Cambridge University Press, 1981.

Stevens, Wallace *Selected Poems*. New York: Vintage, 1959.

Tabbi, Joseph *Cognitive Fictions*. Minneapolis: University of Minnesota Press, 2002.

Tanner, Tony *Henry James: The Writer and his Work*. Amherst: University of Massachusetts Press 1985.

Tolstoy, Lev *Anna Karenina*. Translated by Richard Pevear and Larissa Volkhonsky. London: Penguin, 2000.

Unger, Peter *Ignorance*. Oxford: Oxford University Press, 2002.

Waite, Geoff *Nietzsche's Corpse*. Durham: Duke University Press, 1996.

Walsh, Dorothy *Literature and Knowledge*. Middletown: Wesleyan University Press, 1969.

Williams, Bernard 'Introduction', Nietzsche, *The Gay Science*. Cambridge: Cambridge University Press, 2001.
Truth and Truthfulness. Princeton: Princeton University Press, 2002.

Williams, Raymond *Keywords*. London: Fontana, 1983.

Williamson, Timothy *Knowledge and its Limits*. Oxford: Oxford University Press, 2000.

Wittgenstein, Ludwig *Culture and Value*. Translated by Peter Winch. Chicago: University of Chicago Press, 1984.

On Certainty. Translated by Denis Paul and G. E. M. Anscombe. Oxford: Blackwell, 1969.

Philosophical Investigations. Translated by G. E. M. Anscombe. Oxford: Blackwell, 1967.

Tractatus Logico-Philosophicus. Translated by C. K. Ogden. London: Routledge, 1981.

Yeats, W. B. *Collected Poems*. Edited by Richard J. Finneran. Basingstoke: Macmillan, 1989.

Yeazell, Ruth Bernard *Language and Knowledge in the Late Novels of Henry James*. Chicago: University of Chicago Press, 1976.

Index